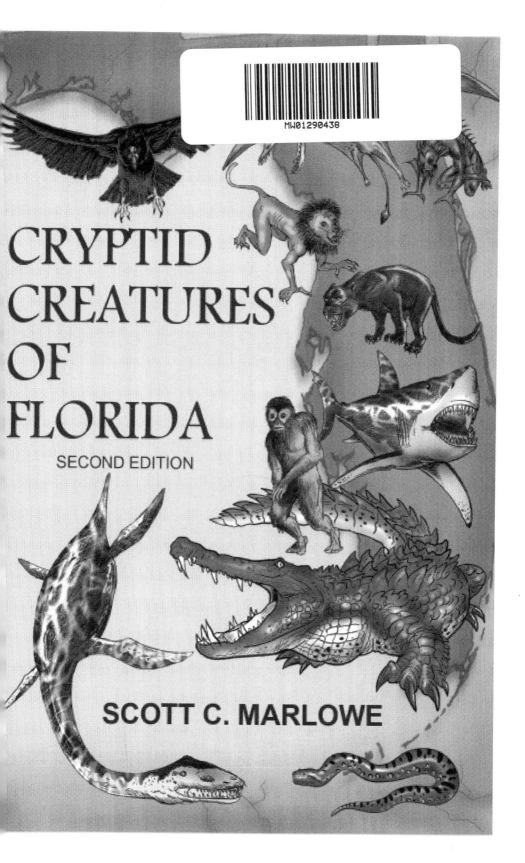

CRYPTID CREATURES OF FLORIDA

SECOND EDITION

SCOTT C. MARLOWE

Cover by Peter Loh

Second Edition published in the United States by
Pangea Press

Pangea Press
514 Winter Terrace
Winter Haven, FL
33881

Copyright © 2014 by Scott C. Marlowe.

ISBN: 978-1495398704

DEDICATION

To Fans of Cryptozoology and the Fellows at Pangea Institute who have indulged my ongoing fascination with unknown animals.

STATE OF FLORIDA AND ITS COUNTIES

1. Escambia
2. Santa Rosa
3. Okaloosa
4. Walton
5. Holmes
6. Washington
7. Jackson
8. Calhoun
9. Bay
10. Gulf
11. Gadsden
12. Liberty
13. Leon
14. Wakulla
15. Franklin
16. Jefferson
17. Madison
18. Taylor
19. Hamilton
20. Suwannee
21. Lafayette
22. Dixie
23. Columbia
24. Gilchrist
25. Baker
26. Union
27. Bradford
28. Alachua
29. Levy
30. Nassau

31. Duval
32. Clay
33. St. Johns
34. Putnam
35. Flagler
36. Marion
37. Volusia
38. Citrus
39. Hernando
40. Sumter
41. Lake
42. Seminole
43. Orange
44. Brevard
45. Osceola
46. Polk
47. Pasco
48. Pinellas
49. Hillsborough
50. Manatee
51. Sarasota
52. Hardee
53. DeSoto
54. Highlands
55. Okeechobee

56. Indian River
57. St. Lucie
58. Martin
59. Glades
60. Charlotte
61. Lee
62. Hendry
63. Palm Beach
64. Broward
65. Collier
66. Monroe
67. Miami-Dade

Contents

Forward

Many years ago, when I was about fourteen, I went to a carnival that had a sideshow featuring a live unicorn. Being a fan of strange and unusual things, I stood in front of the tent marveling at two large, colorful banners depicting a pure white, bearded, equine with cloven hooves and a spiral horn protruding from the center of its head. I wondered to myself "Could such a beast be real? If so, what was it doing in a carnival exhibit instead of being studied at a scientific institution?" I had a choice to make, I could use the last of my money riding the Tilt-a-Whirl or pay fifty-cents and find out the truth about the creature inside the tent. Needless to say, my youthful curiosity forced two quarters from my pocket and I soon found myself inside the tent looking at a live animal standing on a bed of hay behind a canvas enclosure. It was not exactly the creature I had expected, but rather a common billy goat sporting a single, slightly off-center, horn. Although the sideshow banners had greatly exaggerated this live oddity, there were a few elements of truth. The animal did have one horn, cloven hooves, and a beard — but was obviously not a unicorn.

If I had not been willing to take the time, or waste my last two quarters, I would never have known what kind of animal was concealed inside that tent. My curiosity had been stirred by embellished claims painted on sideshow banners which sent me in search of the truth. And even though it had turned out to be just a plain ol' billy goat, it *still provided me with a plausible* answer. In a simple way, my sideshow experience is reminiscent of cryptozoology when it comes to explaining hidden or displaced animals — or cryptid-creatures that conventional science says do not exist despite the number of credible reports. In their quest for truth, whatever it may be, cryptozoologists often tangle with scoffing skeptics while sifting through exaggerations, misidentifications, hoaxes, hallucinations, optical illusions, and myths. While these discouraging factors represent about eighty percent of cryptid sightings, the encouragement for cryptozoologists is the remaining twenty percent containing well-documented and credible sightings. These are the intriguing observations ignored by skeptics and avoided by most conventional scientists.

Do unicorns exist? I don't know because I have never seen one, well, except for that one-horned goat in the sideshow. However, the idea of unicorns had to begin somewhere and all such legends contain a little truth, sometimes more than we expect. Perhaps unicorns became extinct thousands of years ago, like that big ugly coelacanth fish did some 65 million years earlier, that is until 1938 when fishermen began catching live ones. Such discoveries are rain on a skeptic's parade. I say get used to it because there's more strange flora and fauna yet to be discovered on our planet.

Taxonomists, who classify new plant and animal life, enter an average of 1,400 new ocean species into their databases each year. According to the World Register of Marine Species there are 122,500 known ocean creatures and researchers estimate there could be three times as many unknown species. Does this not raise the possibility of discovering a living sea monster? For centuries, humans have reported seeing strange serpent-like creatures in our oceans, lakes, and rivers. Whether seen in Scotland's Loch Ness, Georgia's

Altamaha River, or a newspaper article about a decomposing carcass hooked in 1885 by a ship's anchor in Florida's New River Inlet, witnesses have basically described what sounds like a plesiosaur. There were many species of these prehistoric, long-necked, marine creatures that (according to science) met their end 65 million years ago during the Cretaceous-Tertiary period. Wait a minute, wasn't that when conventional science said the coelacanth became extinct?

Most people do not realize what little we know about the earth's fauna. In 2007 alone, science documented over 18,000 previously unknown species ranging from microbes to mammals. We take it for granted that every animal has been discovered, which is not the case. Unfortunately, many species will likely vanish into extinction before they can be found and studied. Hence the need for cryptozoology which, unlike conventional research, is willing to examine the unknown even if it means investigating Chupacabra sightings in Florida or a giant flaming lizard in Indonesia. As for the flaming lizard, it turned out to be real when explorers discovered the previously unknown species in 2007. Dubbed the "Torch Lizard" because of its reddish-orange head, the four foot reptile is a cousin of the world's largest lizard, the Komodo Dragon — which skeptics claimed was pure myth until 1912 when one was captured.

Florida is full of exotic species, from pythons to iguanas, which have either escaped captivity or were released, illegally, by pet owners. These displaced critters have survived quite well in the state's tropical environment. In *Cryptid Creatures of Florida*, you'll read about extensive research into jaguarundi sightings, an otter-like cat that supposedly ranges from

Central America to the southwest United States. I know this animal exists in Florida because I had my own sighting of one while driving through the Merritt Island Wildlife Refuge. But that's not as bizarre as a displaced kangaroo that became a road kill a few years ago on a stretch of Interstate 95 in Brevard County.

While displaced creatures present a curious mystery to solve, so do those Cryptids of the unknown variety such as the alleged Chupacabra or, Florida's Sasquatch equivalent, the skunk ape or swamp ape. This big hairy biped is my nominee for adoption as Florida's official mascot of the unknown. The foremost researcher of the swamp ape is undoubtedly Scott Marlowe, who has amassed quite a database of sightings in addition to tramping through knee deep swamps searching for evidence. He is objective and fair, meaning he presents evidence for what it's worth — including exposing a few hoaxes. Instead of rehashing old information, Marlowe offers refreshing new theories concerning the possible existence of these creatures.

Scott Marlowe has packed a lot of research and experiences into *Cryptid Creatures of Florida*. This is an overdue book that will delight any reader fascinated by unknown things, particularly those interested in cryptid animals.

- Charlie Carlson

Image from "Strange Florida," by Charlie Carlson, Florida's "Master of the Weird." Courtesy of Charlie Carlson.

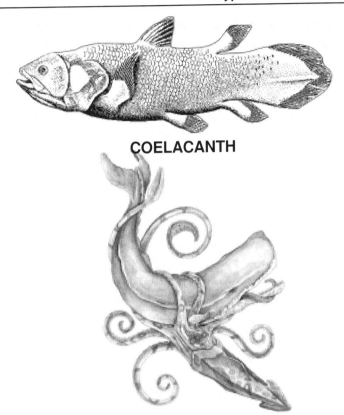

COELACANTH

GIANT SQUID ATTACKING A BLUE WHALE

OKAPI

Introduction

The word "cryptid" describes an animal whose existence in a particular habitat is not scientifically confirmed. A cryptid could be an animal that was known to exist at one time, but is presumed to be extinct (like a pterosaur) or a creature of legend that is known only through folklore and anecdotal evidence (a hydra for example).

The word "cryptid" has also come to be applied to an animal that is known to exist in a specific habitat or location but is found outside of its usual environs or in places that are geographically remote from its normal home range. This is because sightings of the animal are unexpected in locations where it is not normally encountered. This leads to miss-identifications, species confusion and/or speculation that the creature seen is something other than what it actually is (like a "black panther" where these animals are not normally found).

While Cryptids are typically creatures of myth and legend, from time to time, a legendary animal is found to exist in reality — like the coelacanth, giant squid, okapi and mountain gorilla and even the giant panda. All of these animals were, at one time, considered too fantastic or bizarre to be real by the scientific mainstream.

Cryptids occupy a special niche in popular culture. Some have origins in modern urban legends while others have lurked in the shadows for millennia and continue to fascinate us even today.

This book explores Cryptid creatures you'll find in the State of Florida and opens up a new venue of "eco tourism" for those seeking adventure in the outdoors here in Florida. If you enjoy pursuing the odd, strange, unusual or just plain weird things in nature, you'll find this book a great starting place to plan your next eco-safari.

Using this book as your guide, you will travel to areas of Cryptozoological interest here in the Sunshine State along with me, a recognized cryptozoology expert, as your guide. You'll get to "go into the trenches" and search for enigmatic wildlife, learning about their habitats and the environments they live in along the way.

Florida is unique among cryptid locales. We boast, if that's the right word, a counterpart to all of the "Big Five" Cryptids: Bigfoot, The Loch Ness Monster, Chupacabra, Thunderbird, and Dinosauria, here. We also have a few unique Cryptids of our own that wander the more remote places of the state. But beware some of them can even be found right in someone's back yard.

As a peninsular state many cryptid creatures found here are water borne. Still, we have avian anomalies and a wide variety of terrestrial terrors for you to investigate. So, I've organized our Cryptids into those main classifications.

Learn about some of the famous creatures that could be lurking out there as you read through the encounters reported by actual eyewitnesses and researched by my associates and I. Then put on your camos, hip waiters, or scuba gear, and be sure to grab your camera before heading out to search for them for yourself.

PETER LOH 2006

MARINE MONSTERS

SATELITE MAP OF LAKE CLINCH
FROSTPROOF, FLORIDA

Present day aerial view of Lake Clinch (Center) and Ready Lake (on the right). The town of Frostproof is located between the two lakes.

The Lake Clinch Monster

Long before white men arrived in Florida looking for the Fountain of Youth, Native Americans told stories about monsters living in the waters here.

Central Florida was settled in the mid-1800s and a town was established between Lake Reedy and Lake Clinch. The area is notable for its frost-free winters — an important consideration for citrus growers, and the town of "Frostproof" became part of Florida's newly burgeoning orange industry.

*The Mallet homestead overlooking Lake Clinch. Charles Mallet lived here alone as Mrs. Mallet preferred the city lifestyle and keep a residence in Orlando, Florida instead of the "wilds" of Central Florida. The Mallet's Frostproof home has since been demolished. (Photo courtesy of the Frostproof Historical Museum)_*

Orchards were planted and the town grew, but talk about a lake creature had persisted since before settlers arrived. Natives continued to speak of something in the lake and early pioneers, including leading citizens, soon claimed to have seen a thirty-foot long "sea serpent" while boating or from the shore.

On the night of August 30, 1926, 49-year-old Charles M. Mallet stepped out of his simple Florida Cracker style home wearing a bathing suit and carrying a tackle box and bait. Mallett was a businessman, a founder of the town's first bank, and a partner in a prosperous fertilizer and supply company that served the budding orange grove industry.

He was a practical man and tales about a giant serpent inhabiting the lake adjacent to his home did not worry him as he prepared to venture on to the legendary monster's domain.

Before going out to fish, Mallett had told several associates that he would be leaving for Sarasota the following day and absent from his usual haunts during the coming week.

He stopped long enough to wave to a neighbor then made his way down to the public dock.

The old community pier on Lake Clinch from which Charles Mallet launched his boat on that fateful evening of his death. The pier no longer exists.

Like other men in Frostproof, he kept a small boat at the community pier and frequently fished for the largemouth bass that were (and are) abundant in the lake. It was Florida's "monsoon season" and there had been heavy rain that afternoon, but now it was clear skies as Mallett boarded his boat and headed out onto smooth dark water.

A small fishing boat on Lake Clinch similar to that owned by Charles Mallet.

Three days later, on Thursday morning, G. D. Moree cast a fishing line into Lake Clinch from the eastern shore. He reeled it in and snagged something big: a human body.

The features were so mangled that given the state of forensic science in 1926 it might have remained unidentified but for a ring on the corpse's finger; the name faintly engraved on the inside of the band was "Charles M. Mallet".

To confirm the identity, a person was dispatched to see if Mallet had returned from his trip. One of Mallett's employees, C. C. Matthews, discovered the door to the Cracker house unlocked and Mallett's personal effects and suitcase awaiting his return from the lake. There was no doubt that the body was that of Charles Mercer Mallett.

What had happened out on Lake Clinch?

Polk County did not have a medical examiner until the 1970s so an autopsy by today's standards was not performed. It is likely that a physician or district coroner examined Mallett's body. A record of the death has been found in the state's official Death Index (the entry notes a guide number and volume), but if anything more detailed, if it ever existed, seems to have vanished.

With the assistance of modern web resources and research assistance from my friend and associate, Owl Goingback, at Greenwood Cemetery in Orlando, Florida, I was able to locate Mr. Mallett's grave and the burial records associated with it. The funeral home that embalmed Mallett's corpse recorded his death as an "accidental drowning." Newspapers of the day reported the same "official" version of Mallet's death; that he fell overboard, drowned, and his face disfigured by fish. The customary obituary and mention of Mallett's final resting place did not appear in area newspapers. Two weeks later, when a hurricane nearly wiped out Miami, more pressing issues rendered the case all but forgotten.

Paperwork related to Mallet's death might have been lost or destroyed in the storm that ran roughshod over much of the state. In addition, the relatively primitive technology found in towns like Frostproof at the beginning of 20th Century; make a thorough investigation into Mallett's death impractical. Meanwhile, the townsfolk considered other more bizzare possibilities.

Rumors circulated around the town that the monster was

responsible for Mallett's untimely death. Members of the community were loath to discuss this idea with outsiders yet they had seen enough to make the idea seem far from ridiculous.

A few years before the Mallett incident, Frank Whitman was fishing near Coon Slough on the western side of Lake Clinch when a great serpent came up from the water just twenty yards from his boat. He later confided to Orren Ohlinger, one of the town's founders, that, "it was so big and ugly it scared me almost to death."

Whitman must have felt considerable relief, and some trepidation, when Ohlinger said that he believed him — not because of their friendship — but because Ohlinger had also encountered the creature. He went on to say that other townsfolk had been seeing it off and on since at least 1907.

Ohlinger said that the monster had appeared after a heavy rain, rising out of the water some 200 yards from the eastern shoreline. Its body was at least thirty feet long and undulated through the lake. Then it lifted up its head, which was as large as the head of an adult human, three feet out of the water, before disappearing into the depths.

Other sightings made by respectable citizens are preserved in diaries and journals at the Frostproof Historical Society and in private collections of memoirs. Anecdotes have little value as evidence, but a striking aspect of the Lake Clinch stories is the consistency of the creature's descriptions and of the circumstances surrounding its appearance.

When the modern press reported sightings in 1975, 1978 and 2008, the creature was labeled as something akin to Scotland's Loch Ness Monster, but this is incorrect. Popular imaginations (and many cryptozoology buffs) say that "Nessie"

Specifically a plesiosaur features: a long neck, oar-like flippers, and an oval elephantine body. This description never appears in eyewitness descriptions of the Lake Clinch creature. Though each account might contain additional (but revealing) details about the animal, and the encounter may take place in different parts of the lake, the overall serpentine representation of the "monster" is extraordinarily uniform.

Another common feature is that nearly everyone claiming to have encountered the creature did so shortly after a heavy rain. Herpetologists will tell you that snakes like to come out after a storm so that they can drink fresh rainwater. This factor, as well as reports of the creature being about thirty feet long, points to a plausible solution to the Mallet "who done it?" Yet there is more evidence to consider.

The Reader will recall that Mr. Mallett's face was terribly disfigured when he was pulled from the water about sixty hours after his apparent drowning. This is just one aspect of the "official" cause of death inconsistent with today's forensic science.

In warm temperatures, drowning victims will sink as soon as their lungs are filled with water. Depending on the person's clothing, body fat, and other factors, a submerged body may float several feet above the bottom. Mallett was of average build for his age and wore only a lightweight swimming outfit.

A body floats because the gases produced from decomposition are trapped within it, gases that are more buoyant than the water in the lungs. This is similar to the reason a submarine will surface or dive by taking in, or releasing water from, its ballast tanks.

The environment in which a body decomposes affects the

rate of decomposition. A formula called Casper's Ratio states that "if all other factors are equal, then, when there is free access of air a body decomposes twice as fast than if immersed in water and eight times faster than if buried in earth."

Decomposition of tissue begins almost immediately after death, but the speed of its decay in water depends primarily on temperature. When the ambient temperature of the surrounding water is fifty degrees Fahrenheit (10 c.) or higher, the body eventually floats to the surface in five to eight days. The ambient temperature of Lake Clinch during the summer months ranges from the high 70s (21 c.) to low 80s (27 c.) in Fahrenheit degrees.

Although bloating and discoloration occurs within days, very little flesh is lost if the body is found within two to three days – as was the case with Mallett. Fish can mangle a cadaver but it generally takes more time unless the body is in the ocean, where there are big fish, or in places like the Amazon that have denizens like piranhas.

Alligators take their prey underwater and wedge the carcass into a sunken tree or other spot until it "ripens." Gators can't chew and must wrench chunks of rotten meat from the body of its prey after putrefaction occurs. Neither do they seem to have been responsible for the unusual lacerations on Mallett's face.

Several witnesses reported puncture wounds around Mallett's face and the back of his head. These puncture marks reportedly formed an odd crescent-shaped pattern suggesting the shape of a large jaw. These wounds apparently lacked "classic" indicators that designate that they were inflicted post-mortem. (See PubMed "Postmortem wound dehiscence. A report of three cases." Appearing in

Thus the circumstances surrounding the discovery, timing, and condition of Mallett's corpse tends to contradict current modern forensic science thinking.

Every aspect of the Mallett case and the stories about the creature in Lake Clinch fits what we know about large, South American anacondas.

Problems with exotic snakes are nothing new in Florida, where Governor Charlie Crist recently signed off on a python hunt to destroy an estimated 150,000 of these exotic species on state lands.

Many readers will recall the photo of an American alligator killed and subsequently ingested by a python; the serpent only burst open because another alligator bit into the snake after it had swallowed the first.

Is it possible that horrific scenes like these are not just a modern phenomenon? Recent archeological discoveries suggest some intriguing possibilities.

From Flathead Lake, Montana, to the waters of Florida, Native American legends tell of horned serpents and "great snakes".

Not far from Lake Clinch, in Lake Pierce, there is a "hammock", a small, forested area rising above the surrounding marshland, called "Snodgrass Island." The remains of a Mayan trading post were recently discovered there, a find that has been confirmed by the Institute of Mayan Studies in Miami and anthropologists and archaeologists at the University of Florida at Gainesville.

The presence of Mayans in Florida may surprise many people, yet Columbus reported seeing Mayan seagoing canoes in several places around the Florida coastline during his travels. (Robert J. Sharer & Sylvanus Griswold Morley, "The Ancient Maya" Stanford University Press (1994)). Researchers outside of mainstream archeology have long argued that ancient peoples were more widely traveled then is generally believed. There are, for instance, "rune stones" containing glyphs of Mende characters (the Mende are a group of old West African traders) and colossal sculpted heads with arguably African features, which have been found in the Yucatan and Central America, the land of the Mayans and their predecessors the Olmecs. Mayan outposts have also been discovered in Venezuela near the Orinoco River, within the home range of the green anaconda.

A serious excavation of the Snodgrass Island site has not yet been undertaken yet it is somewhat similar to the Mayan settlement of Punta de Chimino in Guatamala, iincluded defensive features. One of them is a moat around the village.

Could it be that the ancient Mayans, who worshiped a feathered serpent, (as did the later Aztecs and other Mesoamerican peoples), brought green anacondas from South America to help protect the trading village at Snodgrass Island by stocking the moat with enormous serpents?

If snakes were a part of the Mayan's defense system, could these exotic animals have found their way into the ecosystem and taken up residence in local lakes long before the modern era? This hypothesis may offer a plausible explanation for indigenous North American tribes passing on tales of great serpents in the lakes and rivers of Florida and elsewhere.

My associate, Robert Robinson, and I went looking for evidence to this affect. While our excursion on to Lake Clinch in Robert's hovercraft did not turn up anything to support this hypothesis, our research into other historical giant snake stories did. I've included another case involving a giant serpent we uncovered in another section of this book.

Nevertheless, the residents of Frostproof were not living in the Stone Age. Most may not have actually seen a living anaconda, but they had access to illustrated books and periodicals and should have been able to connect the South American snake to their "monster" if indeed it resembled one.

Earlier this year, scientists including Dr. Jonathan Bloch a vertebrate paleontologist at the University of Florida, announced the discovery of a new species of giant prehistoric snake native to South America. The fossil remains of the Titanoboa cerrejonensis was found in an open pit coal mine in Columbia near the border of Venezuela. Dr. Bloch estimates that this prehistoric super-snake reached a length of forty to fifty feet and weighed about 2,500 pounds. He also postulates that a warmer climate than previously assigned to the Paleocene permitted the cold-blooded T. cerrejonensis to reach much larger sizes than modern day serpents.

The Titanoboa lived during the Paleocene epoch approximately 60 to 58 million years ago – eons before the appearance of modern man —- so neither the snake nor its fossilized remains are likely to have inspired Native American folklore about giant serpents.

Deceit should always be considered when researching anomalous animals.

Col. Percy Fawcett's highly publicized encounter with a 62-foot anaconda was widely reported in U. S., Newspapers and some might find the sighting of a serpentine monster at Lake Clinch in the same year a suspicious coincidence.

Coi. Percy Fawcett encountered a giant green anaconda while on expedition in South America. Could Charles Mallet have had a similar encounter?

While it is possible that the citizens of Frostproof conspired together to attract attention (and business) to their little town by concocting the account, such a conspiracy and keeping it secret all these years seems unlikely. None of the people that might have been involved in a scheme ever confessed nor are there rumors of a deliberate hoax.

Neither has the creature been given an affectionate nickname like "Champ", the beast in Lake Champlain. Drivers heading towards Frostproof will not be greeted by a chamber of commerce billboard welcoming them to the "Home of Frosty" (or maybe 'Clinchy?'), "Central Florida's Most Beloved Lake Monster." In other words if it was a publicity stunt, it remains a largely un-promoted one.

More to the point, While folklore involving giant snakes exist, there is no physical evidence that one of these giant constrictors was ever captured, killed, or just died of old age and washed up on shore, in the centuries since Mayan influence came to the state. But this is a possibility we should remain open to.

Yet, no photographs or physical evidence – real or faked — that would support the creature's existence have come to light,

Whatever happened to Charles Mallett was certainly strange and older residents of Frostproof might wonder from time to time if a giant snake was responsible. And if it was, where did it come from?

Could it have been the massive descendent of an exotic anaconda? Or, perhaps a living relic of a past epoch when colossal serpents lived and died?

Perhaps most importantly, could the creature or one of its descendants, still be lurking in Lake Clinch today?

The Pensacola Sea Monster

The Lake Clinch creature story is largely unknown. However, another, contemporary sea monster mystery received considerably more notice in the press and attention from cryptozoologists. The story is so strange that it bears repeating here.

On what started out to be a pleasant Saturday morning in March of 1962 near Pensacola Bay, Florida, young Edward Brian McCleary and four of his friends - Eric, Warren, Brad and Larry – planned to dive near the sunken battleship "Massachusetts."

The old battleship wreck lies in about thirty feet of water and can be an unpredictable, if not difficult dive because she lies close to Pensacola Pass — an area that is known among divers for strong currents and poor visibility.

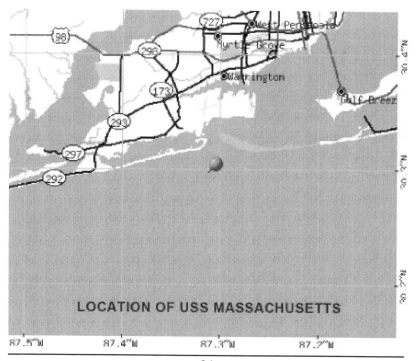

LOCATION OF USS MASSACHUSETTS

There is little background on these young men that turns up in normal investigative channels, but from what information is to be had, they appear to have been fairly "normal kids." Presumably they were active, healthy and outdoor loving young people with a tendency toward finding trouble — like my own kids.

The young men were midway to their intended dive site, paddling out to the wreck in an old rubber Air Force rescue raft, the weather turned threatening (as Florida weather is prone to do). A sudden squall dragged the group further out into the Gulf.

The storm quickly subsided, but a heavy fog settled over the water. Then

"We began to hear strange noises, rather like the splashing of a porpoise,"

. . . recalled McCleary.

The five divers cringed in their rubber raft. McCleary remembers that the mist seemed filled with

"a sickening odor like that of dead fish."

Then, about forty feet away, the young men heard a tremendous splash. Waves reached the raft and broke over its side.

"The noise got closer to the raft,"

said McCleary.

"It was then we heard a loud hissing sound."

This drawing is Edward Brian McCleary's own rendering of the sea animal that attacked him and the four other young men off the coast of the Florida Panhandle.

The boys knew that the sound was not that of any sort of boat nor was it from any sea animal with which they were familiar.

Suddenly they heard another large splash, and through the fog

> *"we saw what looked like a long pole — about ten feet high — sticking straight up out of the water. On top was a bulb-like head. Like a light bulb. Round with a beak on it."*

The neck remained erect for a moment, then bent in the middle and the head dove under the surface of the Gulf. The sickening odor filled the air and then the boys heard a strange, high-pitched squeal from out in the fog.

> *"It appeared several more times,"*

McCleary related later.

"Each time getting closer to the raft."

Beginning to panic, the five young men slipped on their swim fins, and tumbled out of their raft and into the Gulf of Mexico.

"Keep together and try for the ship,"

McCleary yelled.

They made a desperate attempt to reach the portion of the Massachusetts that remains above water. In the back of them, as they raced for the wreck, they could hear splashing and that strange hissing sound.

"We became split up in the fog,"

said McCleary

"From behind me, I could hear the screams of my comrades one by one."

Warren was the first to go. McCleary recalled his frantic call,

'Help me! It's got Brad! We've got to get outta here! We gotta get ..."

Warren's voice was abruptly cut off by a muffled scream.

The three remaining swimmers continued their frantic swim, not knowing how much water separated them from whatever monster it was that pursued them.

Larry was the next to disappear.

"One minute he was there beside me, the next he was gone,"

said McCleary. The two remaining divers dove under to look for their friend but could not see any trace of him.

"Eric got a cramp in his leg"

and called for help. McCleary was able to find him in the fog and wrapped his arms around Eric's neck and continued toward the wreck with his friend in tow. But, a wave broke overt them, separating the two once again. When McCleary surfaced, he saw Eric swimming just ahead of him.

"Right next to Eric that telephone pole-like shape broke the water,"

McCleary stated.

"I got a closer look at the thing just before my last friend went under. The neck was about twelve feet long, brownish- green and smooth looking. The head was like that of a sea-turtle except more elongated, and it had teeth. I could see two small eyes. The eyes were green with oval pupils. There appeared to be what looked like a dorsal fin when it dove under for the last time."

The mouth opened and the monster's neck bent over and the creature

"dove on top of Eric, dragging him under,"

related McCleary.

Screaming and hysterical McCleary actually swam on

"I finally made it to the ship, the top of which protruded from the water, My insides were shaking uncontrollably"

McCleary related. He spent a sleepless night huddled in fear that the creature would return to devour him as it had taken his friends.

Early the next morning, after assuring himself that the monster had left the vicinity,

"I swam to shore from the wreck,"

said McCleary Somehow the young man managed overcome his fright and swim the two miles back to shore in constant fear that the creature would return.

McCleary later recalled flashback slideshow images of reaching the beach, stumbling to a lifeguard tower, and sprawling on his face in the sand before a group of startled teenagers. When McCleary regained consciousness, he was in the Pensacola Naval Base Hospital.

The local newspapers carried the story of the tragedy but they all attributed the boys' death to "accidental drowning." None of the reporters wanted to include the fantastic story of McCleary's escape from the hideous sea monster as related by the survivor. McCleary was told that his story about the sea serpent "was best left unmentioned." However, McCleary would later write his own account of the incident for Fate Magazine.

In the article (May 1965) McCleary says that he asked E. E. McGovern, the director of the search and rescue units, if he believed that the boys had been attacked by a sea monster. "People don't believe these things because they are afraid

The plesiousaur theory for the identity of the Loch Ness Monster is now rejected by most cryptozoologists for a number of reasons, not the least being that it would have bred on land, and being an air breathing creature would be seen more often than it actually is.

to," McGovern admitted. "I believe you, but there's not much else I can do."

Later newspaper articles reported that the body of one of the boys was later found washed up on the beach. An autopsy attributed his death to accidental drowning. The remains of the other three boys were never found.

Paleontology fans will immediately recognize the monster in the story as resembling a supposedly extinct seagoing reptile — the plesiosaur — which is thought by many to be the identity of the mysterious Loch Ness monster of Scotland. However this animal attribution would likely be incorrect as plesiosaurs did not range in North America. However, the plesiosaur did have a counterpart which patrolled the coastal waters of the American continent during the age of the dinosaurs — the elasmosaur.

There are some subtle details in the McCleary story that don't add up to be sure. A search of ancestry.com reveals several Edward McClearys who live, or have lived, in Florida. However, none of their birth dates correspond to the apparent age of the Edward Brian McCleary in the story. A search of the telephone white pages turns up only one Edward B. McCleary living in the Jacksonville area who is about the right age.

Nevertheless I have spoken to people who claim direct contact with McCleary. These individuals assure me that the McCleary of this story does in fact exist but that he will not discuss the matter with anyone. He has apparently suffered from the effects of survivor's guilt leading to a troubled life involving drugs and alcohol. If this is true McCleary has apparently managed to live under the legal radar as a search of the Escambia County and Florida State penal records did not turned up an Edward B. McCleary in their files.

Shortly after the Pensacola incident a minister also reported sighting a creature of nearly identical description from atop a bridge near Panama City, Florida.

Apparently McCleary and this minister have some association with Kent Hovind, an infamous young earth Creationist whose agenda includes proving that man and dinosaur coexist. Assuming this to be true, Hovind's influence would make it easy to dismiss McCleary's story as bunk and attribute the attack to a bull shark and a wild imagination fueled by guilt. Bull shark attacks are regularly reported in the Pensacola area.

But, McCleary and the minister aren't the only Florida residents that report seeing a creature approximating McCleary's description.

Five construction workers in Marathon, Florida also claim to have seen a sea monster of the same ilk some time later while working on a project near the Gulf side of Fat Deer Key. They said that the animal was seen less than 100 yards off shore from them where they were working.

Sightings of sea monsters in Florida waters have also been reported on the Atlantic side of the state. Principally in the Saint Johns River vicinity.

Two navy men stationed at the Jacksonville Naval Air Station and two fishermen reported a "dog headed" sea monster with odd "antennae" appendages jutting out from its head in the water just off the base on two separate occasions. Their description of the creature mimics that of the famed Ogopogo monster, said to be a cadborosaurus, of Lake Okanagan region in Canada.

Another long-necked lake monster," Pinky," is seen from

time to time in the Saint John's River south of Jacksonville, and in a highly publicized signing in the mid-1970s was seen in Lake Monroe near Sanford, Florida.

Stories of water borne monsters like this are relatively common along the Atlantic Seaboard and the Pacific Coast as well as the Gulf of Mexico here in North America. Most, but not all, of these accounts are attributed to wayward Manatees. However, manatees don't have ten-foot long necks and — they are not carnivorous.

Saint Augustine's Giant Octopus

While strolling the beach early one morning in January of 1897 on Anastasia Island, Herbert Coles and Dunham Coretter; two residents of nearby St. Augustine, Florida, discovered something unexplained lying on in the surf. The putrefying blob of flesh was the remains of a huge animal some four feet in height, 23 feet long, and 18 feet across.

In this drawing taken from a photograph of the Saint Augustine "monster" octopus, Dr. Webb inspects the animal's carcass.

Upon hearing of Coles and Coretter's find, a group of investigators from the Saint Augustine Historical Society and Institute of Science went out to Anastasia Island to see for themselves. The team was led by Dr. DeWitt Webb of the University of Florida. Webb quickly determined that the fleshy blob had been on the beach for several days. The examiners also identified segments of what they identified as tentacles.

Jules Verne's famed novel "20,000 Leagues Under the Sea" had been published twenty years earlier. The climax of the fictional book was an attack on the occupants of the submarine "Nautilus" by a giant cephalopod.

In Jules Verne's calssic novel, "20,000 Leagues Under the Sea" the occupants of the submarine "Nautilus" were attacked by a giant cephalopod. Until the giant Octopus was discovered in Saint Augustine, these creatures were considered fiction.

Was this thing on the beach a creature of fantasy that had somehow become reality? Were the "old salt" tales of giant octopus and squid actually true? So, the weird discovery became something of a media event in the periodicals of the time.

Soon the media coverage brought A. E. Verrill, a well-known zoologist at Yale University, to the case. Verrill estimated the size of the creature in its living state at an amazing two hundred feet from tentacle to tentacle.

Verrill rejected Webb's identification of the carcass as that of an octopus and advanced his own theory that the creature was actually a giant squid. Something of a debate between the experts ensued.

A few days after the find, Webb had its carcass moved forty feet away from the water and undertook a detailed examination and necropsy of the body. This, he hoped would resolve the argument over its species, Webb wanted to be sure of the creature's identification. Webb found no cartilaginous "pen" which would have been part of the remains if it been a squid.

Verrill relented and accepted Webb's initial identification of the animal. However, some academicians and biologists continued to quibble over the creature's scientific designation.

In time, the mystery of the St. Augustine "monster" was forgotten. Then in that 1957, marine biologist Forrest G. Wood, Jr. rediscovered the story of the creature in an old newspaper article. Wood was intrigued by the supposed "sea monster," and tracked down the tissue samples from the carcass which Webb had sent to the Smithsonian Institute for posterity.

An actual period photograph of the "monster's" carcass

After studying the tissue samples with new scientific technologies, Wood and Joseph F. Gennaro, Jr., concluded that the body was, indeed, that of a huge octopus.

Not forgetting about the giant cephalopod cousin, the giant squid, in August of 2007 a juvenile giant squid was discovered floating off the Florida Keys near Marathon by North Fort Myers, Florida resident David Stout. The squid was completely intact and measured nearly seven feet long from back to tentacle tip. The squid was taken to the Mote Marine Laboratory for identification and study.

To date, fifteen giant squid have been found in the waters off Florida and the Bahamas — all of them fully grown until the juvenile giant squid was found.

"Molly the Mollusk" a twenty seven foot long giant squid was discovered near New Zealand. She is on display at the Mote Aquarium in Sarasota, Florida. The Mote is the only museum in the United States where you can view Architeuthis dux — the scientific name for the giant squid. The juvenile giant squid is being prepared to go on display there as well.

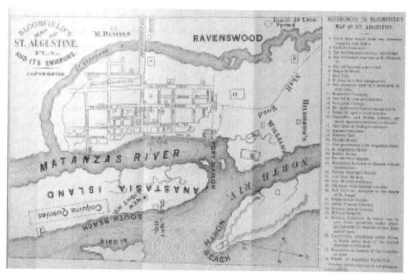

An early tourist map by Max Bloomfield of St. Augustine (circa 1884) depicting principle sightseeing locations from the same general time period in which the Giant Octopus was found -- including Anastasia Island where the remains of the giant beast were found.

Megalodon

The general consensus among mainstream zoologists, marine biologists and paleontologists is that Carcharodon megalodon is extinct. But, several cryptozoologists and some researchers are not so sure. They think that this enormous shark may continue to exist in the deep ocean or perhaps the more remote areas of the Seven Seas.

The discovery of the giant squid, thought to be one of the megalodon's diet mainstays, adds some credence to an array of recent sighting accounts of these giant sharks reported to measure fifty feet or more off the Florida Coast. Scientists at the University of Florida's Natural History Museum speculate that the megalodon went extinct two million years ago because it fed on whales which preceded its extinction due to rapid climatic changes that took place during the Miocene and Pliocene Epochs.

Florida, and in particular the "Bone Valley" area here in the state is well-known for the fossilized teeth that the ostensibly extinct megalodon left behind millions of years ago. But, from time to time a tooth is found which has not been fossilized and is presumed to have belonged to one of these recently living monster sharks. Whale teeth are also common fossil finds.

But, a good number of sports fishermen and charter boat operators have reported seeing a behemoth shark resembling the megalodon in the waters off Florida — particularly in and around the Florida Straits, Tampa Bay and Miami.

Clearly, some of these Megalodon reports may simply be great white shark "fish stories" where the animal's size was miss-estimated or exaggerated by the eyewitness. Still others could be a case of mistaken identity where the real animal seen was actually a whale shark.

I can relate to this possibility having had an encounter with a large shark while deep-sea fishing off Miami as a teenager. I was on board a 55-foot cabin cruiser and have been trolling for large game fish all morning. However the chum attracted a particularly large shark which dogged the boat most of the day until a sudden squall raised twenty-foot waves on Biscayne Bay.

The shark was a monster, but was not nearly as long as the boat. I'm not sure of the species but I am sure that the animal was at least twenty-five feet in length. The shark came alongside the cruiser for time and I could see it easily extended from the stern of the boat to the forward cabin entrance.

While fishermen might be tempted to exaggerate the size of a shark I find the accounts offered by experienced charter boat captains a bit harder to dismiss.

Then, there are accounts like this one that was anonymously e-mailed to me recently:

> *I was attached to the Coast Guard Cutter "Hudson" out of Miami at the time. I don't remember the date, but we had turned a Cuban ship away from American waters a few days before this with a bunch of migrants.*
>
> *A charter boat off the Florida coast called in a Mayday reporting that a very large shark was threatening their vessel a couple of miles out from Miami. The radio operator on the fishing boat said that the shark was at least 50 feet long.*

We were dispatched to investigate and moved in on the shark's reported position so we could identity it. The shark was easy to spot because it cast a gigantic shadow we could make out on the surface of the water which was pretty calm that day.

One of the petty officers spotted the shark's dorsal fin. The Executive Officer measured the shark from dorsal fin to tail with an electronic measuring device and figured that the shark was just under fifty feet long. We could make out the shark's coloration and markings an ID'd the animal as a whale shark.

The ExO called back to the base on the ship's radio and reported that a whale shark has been spotted. The radio operator at the base replied that the fishing boat operator insisted that what they say was not a whale shark and it had a maul and teeth similar to a great white or tiger shark.

A few moments later, we saw the water turn red with blood gushing from the whale shark. Another shark of the same size bit it almost completely through. This second shark was definitely not another whale shark.

Then this new shark came up on the whale shark from below and bit what was left of the whale shark in half. Blood was everywhere. At first, we all thought that the second shark was a really big great white shark.

But, the face of the ExO turned chalk white. He nervously called in for support, "We need more ships and some experts from the oceanographic institute in Miami to identify what this thing is." Then he turned to us and exclaimed, "That's no great white boys!"

A hour or so later, the "Dolphin" arrived on the site with two shark experts on board. A Special Purpose Craft out of Islamorada showed up about 30 minutes after that.

One expert began to take pictures of the shark right away. The ExO asked the experts, "That thing is too big to be a great white. Do you think it could be a Megalodon." The lead shark expert replied, "That's a Meg all right." The Dolphin is an 87 footer and the meg was about two-thirds the length of that ship. The shark was easily a third larger than the SPC-LE.

The lead expert said, "Given this shark's potential for destruction and disruption of the ecosystem, I recommend that we tag it immediately with an ETD (electronic tracking device) so that we know its location at all times, 24/7". He then produced an ETD from his ditty bag, "I brought some tags with me."

The ExO called up to the bridge, "I can't believe I'm saying this, but we have to get closer to that shark." The experts stood in awe. The younger one exclaimed, "What a beauty!"

The captain joined us at the rail and spoke to the lead expert. "Under no circumstances should the Meg's existence be leaked to the general public," said the expert.

The Dolphin caught up to the shark and managed to tag it using a pole so its movements could be tracked.

But, after tagging the meg, it decided to stay under the boat. We got a good look at it because it came along side and rolled to one side. It was so big that even its slightly open jaw could have swallowed two or three of us easily.

The teeth were as large as a fist. It wasn't aggressive at that point, but we got the feeling that it was curious about the boat and its crew. Its large black eye seemed to be sizing us up.

The young expert figured that the shark was considering us for a meal. But, I thought it was just curious because we were strange to it. I mean, it didn't come up on humans before and was just taking all this in. The younger expert exclaimed "This is the most amazing moments of my entire life!"

The shark continued to hover near the ship for a long time. But, then a pod of porpoises was sighted off the ship's stern. The Meg tilted its massive head in the direction of the pod and in two strokes of its tail, was on top of the porpoises.

There was a moment of stunned silence. We watched in horror as the shark attacked the pod rapidly from below and leapt out of the water on top of them as they scattered. At least six porpoises were caught by the jaws of the meg, and four others were crushed by its massive body and tail. It was an awesome, but completely horrifying sight.

After being awestruck for a significant period of time, the experts conferred with the Captain. The older, lead expert said, "I think it is about time that we leave the area. I don't want to see what just happened happen again with people in the area. This shark cannot be allowed anywhere near the coast. Coastal waters must be monitored at all times now. If this shark heads toward the coast and populated areas it has to be killed and preserved for study. The situation could become much too dangerous and we have to avoid the potential for human casualties."

*With that, the Captain called in on the radio.
"This event never happened. It would, I repeat,
it would cause widespread panic and loss of
business to the area," he said. The captain
recommended that coastal authorities be
informed so that they would have time to
prepare for a possible disaster scenario.*

*But no public warning was ever issued. I
thought you ought to know about this.*

Given the circumstances and location this story strikes close
to home and makes me shudder in recalling my own charter
boat encounter.

While my e-mail source chooses not to reveal any names, or
dates, in his account, I did contact several people who I
thought could perhaps verify the story.

I happen to know that the Coast Guard cutters mentioned
are indeed based out of the Miami station and the given size
of these vessels are correct — as the apparent eyewitness
stated.

Each of the cutters has phone lines which connect though a
telephone routing system available to the public. I called
both the Hudson and Dolphin's executive officers and left a
message asking if either ship had been dispatched to
investigate "a large nuisance shark report" within the past
ten years. Neither officer responded to my inquiry.

I am inclined to think it likely that ostensibly extinct sea
creatures like the megalodon could have survived someplace
in the vast oceans on this planet. While the loss of a food
resource, or perhaps even resources, would have impacted
the survival of megalodons as a species, it seems to me that

some of them could have adapted by substituting an alternate, but similar, food source — as the sighting report suggests. It's thought that whale sharks evolved some 200 million years ago. That falls within the known existence of the megalodon.

True, that some species are so specialized that such adaptation isn't likely, it is also true that we know next to nothing about this animal's behaviors and diet preferences.

The even older coelacanth, once thought extinct by mainstream science, was found very much alive off the coast of South Africa in 1938 and again recently in Indonesian waters. We are only now discovering scant details about this animal's life.

With adequate prey, could a few of the giant Megalodon have also survived extinction as has the Coelacanth?

Giant Catfish and Sturgeon

Reports of giant catfish – some large enough to swallow a man – keep surfacing in many places around the world. Actual specimens have been captured in Spain, Vietnam, Germany and Indonesia. Florida too, apparently has its share of these giant "man eaters."

In some cases, the large freshwater animals are said to have capsized canoes and small boats. Fisherman plying their hobby on large bodies of freshwater like Lake Okeechobee, Lake Kissimmee and other Florida waterways report sightings of these fantastic finned monsters.

Perhaps the most likely reports of giant catfish come from Lake Tarpon where eyewitness accounts tell of a giant "monster" with a length between ten and thirty feet with a head shape resembling a dinosaur. Most report it as shaped like some sort of a large reptile. Some reports state that the animal is able to walk on land as well.

"Tarpie" has been spoken of in local Native American legends for centuries. Indeed, there is one such legend that asserts that people foolish enough to enter the creature's domain may never return.

Many locals suggest that Tarpie is a giant catfish. Skeptics say that this is nonsense because catfish are bottom-dwellers that aren't likely to be seen near the water's surface.

Although we do have an exotic species of (considerably smaller) walking catfish in Florida, it isn't likely that one of these could exit the lake and carry away a fully grown man or woman — as Tarpie has been said to do.

Alligators and manatees have been suggested as the source

for the Lake Tarpon monster sightings, but these culprits are not likely as they would be easily recognized by lake shore residents.

Those that favor the fantastic suggest that Tarpie is a descendent of one of the elasmosaur, like the creature described by Edward Brian McCleary, and say that the creature accesses the lake through an underground cave system. Other Tarpie fans steadfastly hold to the giant catfish explanation.

But, to date at least, I have not seen or heard of a convincing catch or even a photo of Tarpie or of any other of these gargantuan Siluriformes.

But, giant catfish aren't the only enormous finned wonders said to inhabit Florida's lakes and rivers.

The Tampa Tribune ran a story – with photographic evidence – about an enormous sturgeon washing up on the shores of Tampa Bay.

Near the mouth of the Suwannee River reports of giant sturgeon, perhaps not as large as this one, are said to jump into fishing boats and come flying out of the water's surface every year.

While I hear stories like this all time, called in to me, I have not received any reports that can be substantiated or confirmed by a third party. Of course, I'm skeptical and when I ask for verifiable proof from these dubious anglers of their "fish story," I usually get a dial tone as a reply.

But, I have to say that, as a caviar fan, I'm sorely disappointed that our local sturgeon is not known for the quality of its roe — much less its size.

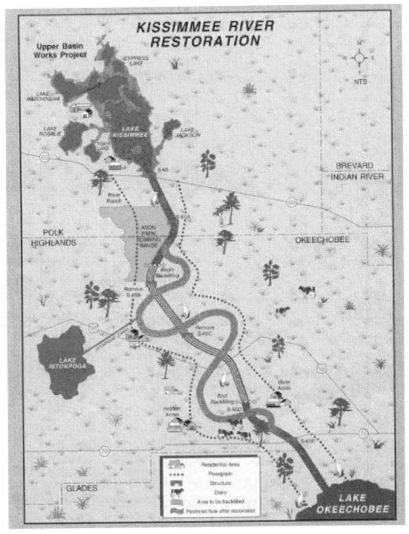

The Kissimmee River system where many of the reports of Giant Catfish in Florida originate.

Giant Alligators

Local legends here in Central Florida is that, at one time, the area was home to the Colusa tribe. One of the tribal leaders had chosen to locate his clan on a lake in what is now Lake Wales, Florida. The area chosen had the advantage of high ground in an area which offered fresh water and good fishing. An added advantage was close proximity to Iron Mountain — the highest point in Florida — and as such was the sacred place of their Sun God.

Cufcowellax, the chief, and his tribe were happily living at this place for years until a massive bull alligator also decided to make the lake his home.

The gator soon became a problem for the Indians as it started to raid the Indian village nightly and carry off anyone he could catch. So, the tribe became terrorized by this "evil spirit" that lived in their lake.

Cufcowellax was endowed with great physical prowess and courage and enjoyed considerable stature among his people as a warrior and as a ruler. So to save his people from the marauding gator, Cufcowellax decided to kill the great reptile. Cufcowellax had his tribal shaman and elders beseech the Great Spirit to protect him and then he set out to find the monster.

Upon locating the animal, he attempted to engage it in a fearsome battle as his people looked on. Although many days passed, Cufcowellax could not catch the alligator. Then, finally one morning, the chief came upon the creature on the northwest shore of the lake as it was dragged another of his victims into the lake.

According to the legend, Cufcowellax fought the alligator on shore and in the lake for nearly a month. At the climax of the

battle, Cufcowellax was dragged under the water by the great beast while still fighting. Soon, the churning water calmed and the water of the lake turned red with blood.

The people watched the surface of the lake fearing that their great chief had perished. But, their fear was replaced with relief when they observed Cufcowellax rise back out of the lake.

Apparently the battle was so fierce that the earth shook — opening a small pond near the large lake where the fight took place. The Indians named the pond "Ticowa" and buried Cufcowellax on the shore nearby when he passed away some time later. The burial site is said to be sacred to the Native Americans.

The media here in the state dubs any alligator greater than twelve feet in length a "giant." But alligators typically grow to this size and frequency and are anything but fantastic monsters.

"Maximo" is a Giant crocodilian measuring fifteen feet-three inches in length, and ways 1,250 pounds. This "giant" can be found at the St. Augustine Alligator Farm — along with two albino cousins,

There is an urban legend about a giant alligator associated with new construction at the Orlando international Airport found by a construction crew working for the Florida Power & Light company.

The story goes that the crew was putting in lines for an addition to the airport and found an eighteen foot-two inch long alligator hiding in a culvert.

However Florida Power & Light (FPL) denies this claim and the photo associated with it which made the rounds on the Internet and the fall of 2002.

While driving west along US Route 41 and 2005, just east of Ochopee, Florida with three of my sons on one of our road trips we encountered a small traffic jam. Because of gridlock was a dead alligator which had been run over, judging from the damage to its body, by a large delivery truck.

This was no small gator. The animal stretched from the shoulder of one side of the two-lane road to the other making it about twenty-four feet in length. Apparently the alligator had been trying to cross the road from one drainage ditch to another when it was struck.

Although tragic for the alligator, the sight was something quite comical as a carload of Oriental tourists had pulled to the side so that the occupants could take countless snapshots of the accident scene.

Above: period illustration, Native Americans in Florida grapple with a giant alligator threatening their tribe. Below: Map of "Spook Hill" in Lake Wales, Florida. Site of Cufcowellax's battle with his Giant Alligator.

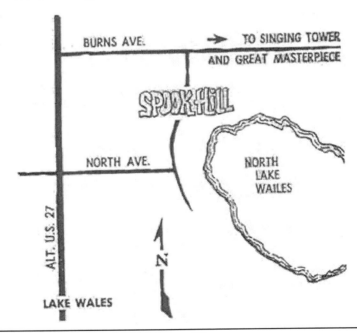

The Giant Juno Worm

Scuba diver and documentary videographer, Jay Garbose, filmed a strange creature off the Florida coast near Juno Beach in Mid-April of 2007. Garbose has filmed for National Geographic and The Discovery Channel (among other cable producers) in the past and has traveled all over the world during his film making career so he's seen many a sea-going denizen.

Garbose discovered a giant, ten-foot long, worm while on a dive that he first thought was some sort of sea cucumber — until he saw the creature's entire length.

Friends of his that work at the Smithsonian weren't sure what the animal was, but thought it might be some sort of Nemertean Worm. (A few odd characteristics of the filmed creature aren't exactly right for an easy identification.)

"I was diving on Juno Ledge, about a mile off Juno Beach. It's sort of grey and putty like and very smooth and taffy-like in the way it stretches. I ... dubbed it the 'living intestine.'" Says Garbose.

If the animal is finally identified as a Nemertean Worm, that designation is both fitting and descriptive of these odd invertebrates. So, for now, the creature is simply an "undescribed" species — thus making this worm a cryptid animal until is scientifically identified, described and presumably dubbed a "Nemertea garbosei."

Nemertea are a group of invertebrate ribbon worms sometimes called "proboscis worms." There are about 1,400 species most of which are marine animals. A few live in fresh water most in salt water. There are also a couple of terrestrial forms. They are known to exist throughout the world.

Most Nemerteans are small creatures, some of which measure a fraction of an inch, but some are known to be over 98 feet in length. The average length of these worms is under a foot. However, a few sighting reports have put specimens at up 200 feet in length. This would make these Worms the longest animal in the world — besting the great blue whale, the longest known vertebrate, which measures about 98 feet when fully grown.

And some skeptics say that "all the big cryptids have been found." Ahh, yea right!

Lake Worth Sea Monster

For four years, Gene Sowerwine, a Palm Beach area resident, filmed a strange animal cavorting in the Lake Worth Lagoon near Singer Island.

During this time, Sowerwine apparently tried to interest a number of cryptozoology experts, including "The Leading Cryptozoologist," Loren Coleman in his "Sea Monster" only to have the footage dismissed as a manatee by everyone he showed it to — most with an "irritated yawn."

Frustrated, Sowerwine resorted to putting a few tantalizing clips of his four hours of video up on the Internet.

Eventually, all of Sowerwine's back stage promotion finally caught the attention of MonsterQuest producers who captured several stills from the video showing some of the more unusual physical features of the monster — including a trident-shaped tail. These were sent on to me in the hope that I'd see something more interesting than manatees frolicking in the intercoastal waterway.

Indeed, the trident tail was interesting — if not misleading — but I very quickly realized that the tail belonged to a manatee injured by the propeller of a careless boater.

However, there was also a blurred photo of what looked like the head of what seemed to be another animal among the manatees. Sowerwine insisted that we were seeing the humps, tail and head of one type of animal. But, I wasn't so sure of that.

On one of my many rounds on Stock Island near Key West, where the commercial fishing fleet docks to deliver their goods, I ran into a salt that told me he had seen Caribbean

In the MonsterQuest television show about the Lake Worth "Sea Monster" graphic artists attempted to render the two animals responsible for the creature's sighting as one animal so that it resembled the creature appearing in the above illustration.

Monk Seals out on some destitute islands in the Caribbean near their fishing grounds.

Now, the West Indian Monk Seal (AKA "Caribbean Monk Seal") had recently been declared "extinct" by U.S. authorities in 2005. The last confirmed sighting being sixty years prior to the official notice of the demise of their species.

I began to wonder if the animal that I saw in Sowerwine's video still could be a monk seal that had somehow survived in the company of these sea cows. Manatees being vegans and seals being carnivores, there didn't seem to be a reason, in terms of food resources, that the two different species would be incompatible.

So, I contacted Rose Dunn, the MonsterQuest Associate

Producer that was responsible for the episode they had decided to shoot about this "cryptid." The next thing I knew, I was on board with their team.

Not totally sure of my animal attribution, I asked to include Dr. Ed Petuch, a Marine Biologist and Geologist at Florida Atlantic University who is both a friend and colleague to get his take on the images.

I was asked by Rose not to "compare notes" with Ed and let him come to his own conclusions. Having heard some accounts of Hooded Seals seen in the US Virgin Islands and of two hooded seals that were found in and around the Palm Beaches (one up in Martin County and the other two miles north of The famed Breakers hotel) on his many travels in search of new fossil mollusk species — Ed's passion — Ed offered yet another possibility after viewing the same photo that piqued my interest.

Ed also offered a viable explanation for an arctic animal to be so far out of its normal habitat. The extinction of the monk seal in this part of the world left a hole in the fauna that global climate change conditions were helping another species of the same genus radiate into.

We had a story to tell.

So, filming dates, or dates to be more exact, were set and we were off and filming once Rose lined up Martine DeWit, an associate research scientist with the Florida Fish and Wildlife Conservation Commission who insisted that the animals seen in Sowerwine's footage were — not surprisingly — manatees.

The show first aired in April of 2007 and a barrage of hate mail, Internet blog challenges and irate phone calls quickly followed — all decrying Ed and I for endorsing "a

—

A drawing of the West Indian Monk Seal now thought to be extinct.

preposterous claim" that there was a seal amongst the manatees. One letter went so far as to state that "Any fool could see that the creatures were manatees, and that Ed should be ashamed for putting his professional reputation on the line to back up a nut job like Marlowe."

Fortunately a short time later a Hobe Sound Newspaper carried a news item that a Bearded Seal was seen in the vicinity of the Inlet there. A little while later, a Channel Five News helicopter from Palm Beach clearly filmed the wayward pinniped in Lake Worth.

Ed and I were wrong about out our species attributions, but we were totally right about the animal's genus. Vindicated, there actually WAS a seal hanging out with a wandering group of manatees, the nasty comments stopped.

The "rest of the story" came a year later, due in part to the exceptional cold spell last winter. Countless manatees huddled in the drain chancel hear the Florida Power and Light Riviera Beach Power Plant to keep warm in the discharge from the power generators. One of the sea cows stood out — the one with the distinct trident tail!

Mystery solved. All of the experts weighing in on the MonsterQuest show had been right!

Well, I suppose that, if our manatees can migrate north to the Hudson River and beyond, we can tolerate one more snow bird (or is it "Snow Pinniped?") hitching a ride with them to winter in the warm waters here.

The Muck Monster

No sooner had the furor from the Lake Worth Sea Monster die down than another mysterious ripple in the surface of Lake Worth conjure up rumblings of yet another cryptid creature haunting Palm Beach.

This time it was City Commissioner, Bill Moss, who sounded the alarm. Apparently fueled by all the sightseers wanting to see the "monster" for themselves, Moss proposed that the city revamp a new pier built nearby into a tourist hot spot where the public could view the "Muck Monster."

Trying to capitalize on monster mania is nothing new. "Bigfoot hunters" have been making money off rumors of the "Big Hairy Guy" for years. So now it looks like a city commissioner is poised to do the same with an as yet unseen animal hovering below the surface of the lake.

Moss proposes to install a "muck monster viewing telescopes" on the pier in the hope that "Mucky" will attract more tourists and local thrill seekers to the city's waterfront.

Although still unseen, Mucky's underwater dance has been caught on tape by the LagoonKeepers organization (who also named the creature "the "Muck Monster") and aired both locally and on some national monster friendly networks.

Well, Mucky has one thing in common with Bigfoot, "We sped up on it to catch up to it and it just dove down. Every time we get ten feet of it, it would just disappear." says Greg Reynolds of the Lagoonkeepers.

What could it be?

In all likelihood, the animal behind these sightings is some

In all probability, the "Muck Monster" is actually a ray fish.

ray fish. My uncle, a longtime resident of Riviera Beach, used to swim daily in Lake Worth. Kurt Carstens (my uncle) had been a Dutch Merchant Marine in his youth and was not a stranger to the sea or its many life forms.

Kurt told me of several encounters he had with rays in the lake. He even caught one on hook and line once from the fishing area off the Singer Island causeway. When they swim near the surface, large rays can make swirls in the water's surface very similar to those associated with Mucky.

However, many sea creatures that frequent murky brackish water inlets like those in Lake Worth can do the same — including more monstrous animals.

Mucky's actual animal identity will probably be debated for some time. Unlike the manatees and seals that turned out to be the "sea monster" in Lake Worth previously, this creature appears to travel alone and it is far more camera shy.

Whatever Mucky is, he or she has certainly got people talking and out observing while Reynolds is cracking jokes "Maybe Nessie's taken to vacationing in South Florida!" — All the way to the bank.

The Sea Devil

Most of the time sea monster's found here in Florida can be easily related to known animals — either zoologically or paleontologically recognized. But occasionally we come across a creature so bizarre that it defies a simple explanation.

Frankly, I'm not sure how to classify the next creature we will discuss. It was ostensibly found in the sea and has some associated sealife characteristics, but the eyewitness description also attributes bird-like and mammalian traits to this animal odd ball.

Robert Schneck was "poking around in some old newspapers" when he came across this article about a Florida "sea monster" appearing in the September 16, 1896 edition of the Logansport Journal of Indiana.

Schneck passed his find along to my friend, Charlie Carlson, Florida's "Master of the Weird" who then sent the piece on to me.

CAUGHT IN FLORIDA.

Marine Monster That is Part Fish, Part Bird, Part Animal. Sea serpents are becoming too cornmon, and when Florida people decided to produce a marine monster the serpent famiily was ignored and the Diabolus Maris was produced.

The picture which is presented was made from a drawing sent to the Kansas City Journal by Capt. George Bier of thc United

States navy. The animal was caught off the\
coast of Florida at Mantazas Inlet in 72 feet
of water.

It was caught on a hook and line and when
dragged aboard the boat was full of fight. In
order to preserve the strange mouster it was
found necessary to kill it, for it was so
vicous that it could not be handled.

This remarkable relic of the antedeluvian
monster seeined to be part bird, part fish
and part animal. Capt. Bierr described it as
follows;

"It has no scales, although it can swim. A
portion of its body is covered with hair and
when it wants to fly it inflates two wind bags
behind Its wings. This inflation is tbough its
gills, which are situated on its breast. It
stands upright on fts feet, which are shaped
like hoofs. Its face and body are more
human than like anything else, and its
mouth is like that of a
raccoon, garnished with two rows of teeth. It
stood about 20 inches high and strutted like
a roostcr."

After its capture the monster was christened
Diabolus Maris, and was transferred to
Tampa, Florida, where it has since been on
exhibition. Naturalists who have sèen it can
find no othér name for It, and its like has
never been seen before.

Captain Bier's own drawing of the "Diabolis Maris" as it appeared in the Logansport Journal of Indiana in 1896.

Some fish bave fins that resemble wings, can be used for fling, but fish dô iiot wear hair. The presence of legs argues that it is not a fish, and its ability to live tinder wnter and the gills prove that it is not a bird.

There is no known seagoing mammal or fish or any other recognizable beast that readily resembles the creature as illustrated by Captain Bier.

Schneck suggests that "the monster is the dried body of a skate (see photo left) with its fins trimmed, balancing on the legs of a goat or piglet,"

Presumably Captain George Bier is the same as the Confederate States commander, George Henry Bier, of the blockade runner ship "Greyhound." The Greyhound was built in Liverpool in 1863 and was delivered to the Confederacy on January 5, 1864 on her maiden voyage, The ship was stationed in Bermuda.

On 9 May 1864 the Greyhound sailed out of Wilmington, North Carolina and famously captured next day by the USS Connecticut, her fame was earned because her passengers included the mysterious "Mrs. Lewis," A.k.a., Miss Belle Boyd — the famed Confederate spy.

The Connecticut was commanded by Acting Ensign Samuel Harding, Jr., USN, who took the Greyhound to Boston. However Harding was seduced by Miss Boyd and persuaded

Bier's "Creature" was likely a sea skate of similar type to this specimen and not an unknown "monster."

to let Captain Bier escape. Bier made his way from Boston to Canada and freedom. Harding was dismissed from the Union Navy in disgrace. History buffs may remember that Harding married Belle Boyd sometime later in England.

According to the Register of Commissioned and Warrant Officers of the United States navy on page 110 confirms that he was a midshipman at the US Naval school. This entry is dated 1848.

Bier is buried in the Key West Cemetery and, according to the tombstone, passed away in 1905. So, it appears that George Bier and George Henry Bier are one and the same person. So we've can verify that the person reported in the Journal article was real and his existance fits the time frame and service background mentioned in the news item.

Assuming that the sighting report was not intended as a contemporary hoax, we can turn our attention to the creature.

If we ignore the wings and spindly legs, we could presume that the animal is a seal. The face, body and tail (sans the wings and legs) does resemble one. Fishermen and surfers have sighted pinnipeds in and around Matanzas Inlet recently and back at the time of this report the Caribbean monk seal is still ranged here in Florida.

But seals don't have gills, nor are they only twenty inches in length when grown.

More to the point an experienced captain like Mister Bier would presumably have recognized a common seagoing mammal — even in the 19th century – and have been able to distinguish between a known animal and a "sea monster."

Going back to Bob Schneck's idea for a moment, a sea

going skate does resemble the drawing of Captain Bier. And, in all probability, the creature was a skate. However, skates don't stand upright on their "legs" and walk.

So what is the Sea Devil? Is it a case of mistaken identity or is it some as yet unknown denizen of the deep?

The Three-Toed Monster

1947 was not a good year for the west coast of Florida. A severe outbreak of Red Tide algae choked the Gulf of Mexico from the Florida Panhandle down to Venice Beach. In the Tampa Bay area the carcasses of dead and dying fish, birds and seagoing mammals where everywhere leaving the water and beaches unusable because of the sickening stench. The Red Tide problem lingered for quite some time. So, it affected vacationing beach goers and local water-loving folks who were compelled to avoid the Gulf Shore for months. Fortunately, after the Red Tide passed and the air cleared, the beach lovers were able to return to enjoy the surf and sand later in the year. Unfortunately, at least according to the stories told to me, so did a mysterious "monster."

Clearwater, Florida was a small city of around 15,000 residents In February of 1948. At 3:30 in the morning, a local couple, who had been "parking" in an area of Clearwater Beach known for privacy — suitable for adult activities — observed a creature coming out of the Gulf below the sand dunes near where they were parked.

At first, the two young people thought the animal was a whale that had beached itself in the shallows. But, they soon realized that this 'creature' was actually hauling itself out of the water and on to land and moving along the shoreline.

The near-hysterical couple quickly made their way to the Sheriff's office where they reported the encounter.

Since Clearwater was a small town, and everybody knew everybody else, the couple was taken quite seriously and an investigation was promptly mounted. At dawn, a small posse, that included the witnesses, began a search of the area of beach area where the creature was seen. The group soon

Above: A photograph of the mystery tracks left by the Three-Toed Monster on Clearwater Beach in 1948.

Below: A picture of a three-toed dinosaur track from Dinosaur Valley State Park in Glen Rose, Texas. The reader will clearly recognize the similarity between the two tracks.

found strange animal tracks measuring nearly 14 inches long and 15 inches across coming up out of the water, following the shore line for about two miles. Then the trail finally disappeared back into the Gulf.

The tracks were photographed and casts were made of them. Animal experts who were later consulted said the creature that had made them had to be nearly 2000 pounds in weight to have left such deep footprints. But, nobody knew what animal known at the time could have made them.

The prints featured three distinct "toes" and resembled the fossil tracks left behind by long extinct sauropod dinosaurs like those seen in Dinosaur Valley outside of Dallas, Texas near Glen Rose and elsewhere.

Over the next several weeks, additional footprints were found on Clearwater Beach and later in the year about 40 miles inland along the Suwannee River a good bit north of Clearwater.

The continued "sightings" eventually caught the attention of zoologist, Ivan T. Sanderson in New York City. Sanderson decided to personally investigate the mystery animal himself and spent several weeks in Florida on expedition searching for the beast -- or at least clues to its identity.

Eventually, Sanderson wrote a report on his research and somewhat unfortunately, stated that the animal's tracks resembled those of giant extinct penguins. Specifically the Pachydyptes ponderosus, known from fossil finds in New Zealand from the late Eocene (37 to 34 MYA) reaching a height of about 5 feet and weighing around 220 pounds. Or, the Anthropornis nordenskjoeldi that lived 37-45 million years ago which reached 5 feet 7 inches in height and weighed in at 200 pounds. Again, found in fossil formations from Seymour Island off the coast of Antarctica to New Zealand. The Emperor Penguin, of today, for comparison purposes, is just under 4 feet tall by comparison.

Sanderson privately thought it was possible that the extinct birds might still exist, But his public statement was only intended to describe the creature's penguin-like feet -- not that the animal being seen actually was a penguin.

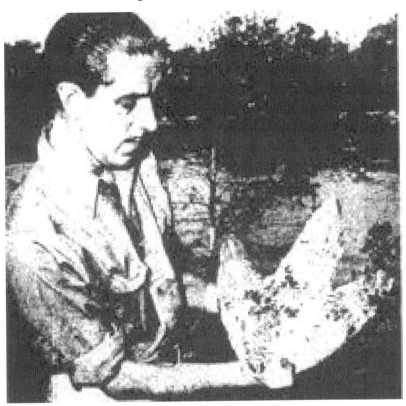

Ivan T. Sanderson examines a Florida Three-Toe track during his 1948 expedition in search of the Monster

Of course, the media jumped all over Sanderson's off hand remark and immediately pronounced the creature a Gigantic Penguin complicating the issue considerably and rendering the search for the animal something of a "Fool's Errand" in the general public's perception.

Giant penguins based upon the fossil discoveries previously mentioned appear in *At the Mountains of Madness* by H. P. Lovecraft. First serialized in the February, March and April 1936 issues of Astounding Stories these penguins are described as being in a fictitious Antarctic underground environment and their presence is given a relatively plausible explanation.

However, such giant birds were, according to the fossil record, only found in the South Pacific and were not contemporary with human populations and were certainly not as tall as the witnesses were reporting for the Clearwater creature.

But, I'm getting a bit ahead of myself here.

Through the spring months and early summer, people continued to find the weird animal tracks on Clearwater Beach. Then, In July of 1948, two student pilots from the Dunedin Flying School reported a mysterious creature in the water near Clearwater Bridge. They described it as resembling "a furry log with a head like a large boar with legs like a giant alligator."

The aviators, George Orfanides and John Milner, were out on a practice flight when they saw the creature. Both men claimed to have seen the monster in the shallows near the bridge off Hog Island.

When the fliers returned to the airfield, and reported in to their instructors at the air school; Mario Hernandez and Francis Whillock, decided to go back up and search for the creature themselves.

They too spotted the monster wading in the shallows and splashing around. Both men said that the animal had enormous webbed arms and powerful legs with a 15 to 20 foot long body length and covered in greyish hair.

The pilots all told their tale to the local newspapers that afternoon adding another anecdote to the legend of the three-toed monster..

Then, a couple of vacationers from Milwaukee who were visiting Tarpon Springs on a fishing trip, rented a boat to cruise around the islands to fish and relax in the sun. Late in the day, these two vacationers came ashore on one of the small cays to cast their nets into the water.

As the man was preparing his gear, his wife went beachcombing. While strolling the beach, she noticed that there was something large, and gray in color hiding in the sea-grape plants. She walked toward it. Her husband saw what was happening and yelled for her to run back towards him. Looking back, she saw a huge creature scrambling to the nearby surf. The creature dashed into the water, and swam away creating a large wake until it finally disappeared under the water.

The now thoroughly terrified couple returned to the mainland to tell their story, describing the creature as at least 15 to 20 feet in length, and had a head like a giant rhinoceros with no neck. It was covered in a thick, stringy grayish hair, and had two enormous flippers for the front appendages with three claws. They added that it had dark, greenish-yellow eyes and a long slit for a mouth. They also said that it had strong reptile-like legs -- having witnessed it diving into the surf.

The duo had no knowledge of the other reports of the monster. This only made their encounter even more compelling to the local media.

However, the descriptions given of the creature by the eyewitnesses did provide a somewhat better perspective on what was actually being seen.

The animal could not have been an alligator or crocodile. Nearly everyone would immediately recognize those iconic Florida denizens. They also don't have three-toes and their trail would include drag marks between their left and right feet from their tails.

The traits that were described better fit the extinct Toxodon. However, that attribution too had quite a few problems.

The Toxodon, although known from fossils obtained by Charles Darwin himself in Uruguay in the 19th century, is an extinct

Artist's conception rendering of the Toxodon

mammal of the late Pliocene and Pleistocene epochs (2.6 million to 16,500 years ago). The animal was indigenous to South America, and appears to have been fairly common. However, the Toxodon was around 9 feet in body length, a height of about 5 feet, with an estimated weight of roughly 3,300 pounds. The creature resembled a heavy rhinoceros, but it had a short and hippopotamus-like head and a light covering of hair. It also had three-toes, but not "flippers" for limbs.

The toxodon was first believed to have been amphibious like crocodilian, but was later determined to be entirely terrestrial like the elephant and rhinoceros. Florida did have its own counterpart to the Toxodon, the Teloceras, during the Miocene Epoch but that animal had a horn, which the eyewitnesses do not ascribe to the monster they saw, but it did not have three toes like the toxodon. But both had legs like a sauropod and are also extinct.

On August 17 of 1948 things got even stranger when a deacon at the First Baptist Church in Chiefland, Florida saw the creature. Rev. Nathan Hayes and some friends were picnicking on the banks of the Suwannee River when they saw a massive, large object floating in the water. Hayes thought it was a "big log," but he soon noticed that it was floating upstream against the flow of the river and moving in "an erratic manner." Hayes in a few of his colleagues took a rowboat out on the river to get a better look. Clearly not a log, the weird creature quickly dove under water when the boat approached it and disappeared with some "snorting and grunting like that of a ferocious beast."

Then on August 20th a local woman, Mary Belle Smith, was fishing on the river in the same general area where the Hayes group had their encounter near the Route 19 bridge at Fanning Springs. Ms. Smith saw a large, blunt-shaped head "the size of a baby elephant's head" come up out of the water in front of her. The creature snorted and made "a strange hissing sound" and then started swimming upstream past the bridge where it disappeared out of sight.

On the 21st, a local trapper named Martin Sharpe heard splashing sounds in the Okefenokee Swamp, a little south of the Georgia State Line with Florida in the evening. When he investigated the source of the noise using a flashlight, he daw a great dark figure in front of him. The creature made "fearful, guttural moans and howls. Then it turned around and galloped away into the swamp."

So it is little wonder that, given the newspaper accounts and unusual descriptions of the beast, zoologist, or in this case I should say "cryptozoologist," Ivan T. Sanderson decided to personally investigate these "monster" sightings.

Later that year, while flying above the Suwannee River in a twin engine airplane belonging to the *New York Herald-Tribune* on October 19, 1948, Ivan Sanderson and pilot Lloyd Rondeau, saw the strange beast that had been harassing the local population from Clearwater Beach north to the Florida State Line. About 500 feet above the Suwannee Gables, a section of river winding its way to the Gulf of Mexico, both Sanderson and Rondeau witnessed a 12-foot long and 5-foot wide creature that had large flipper-like limbs that made a considerable wake as it swam.

The creature was of grayish-yellow coloration. Surprised at their luck in sighting the "monster" the duo made several passes over it to double check their observations. Unfortunately, the creature quickly disappeared into the darkened water. At this point, Sanderson resolved to either capture the beast or at least take photographs of it.

Sanderson planned his Florida expedition for November of

1948 to do further research and attempt to capture the creature or take a picture of it. He spent two weeks studying plaster casts of the tracks, interviewing eyewitnesses and hunting for the beast.

Unfortunately, while Sanderson did gather a good bit of anecdotal evidence and the tracks that the creature left behind, the animal -- whatever it was -- avoided capture and failed to show up for its photo opportunity, much to Sanderson's chagrin.

For the next decade, footprints continued to turn up at Clearwater Beach and the surrounding areas periodically. But, no one was ever able to capture the creature that made them on camera.

Sanderson passed away in 1973 never having solved the mystery of the Florida Three-Toe Monster.

Then, in 1988, a fellow named Tony Signorini stepped forward with the claim that he and his employer at Auto Electric, Albert Williams, created a hoax by crafting metal feet resembling dinosaur tracks Signorini had seen in a National Geographic article and attaching them to a pair of tennis shoes using the equipment at the his repair shop.

According to Signorini's story, he and a companion rowed along the shore in the middle of the night in a small boat, stopping at a likely spot so that Signorini could get out and wander along the beach wearing the "track shoes" and then get back into the boat leaving behind the mysterious tracks. The next morning, a cohort in the hoax would report the "sighting" to the authorities or newspapers.

Signorini retained the metal shoes and put them on for the photo shown on the next page to prove he was the one and only Florida Three-Toed Monster for Jan Kirby of the St. Petersburg Times.

Needless to say, Signorini is likely to have been the culprit responsible for at least some of the mystery track "discoveries." But the fact remains that there were just way too many tracks in too many places for him to have been responsible for of them. More to the point, there were many credible witnesses and not just a few of Signorini's cohorts who actually saw an animal — including Ivan Sanderson himself -- and not Tony Signorini lumbering around with cast iron dinosaur feet attached to his shoes.

Tracks had been found on steep embankments which would have been very difficult, if not impossible, for Signorini wearing such a get up to have traversed.

So, at least part of the Florida Three Toe Monster story in spite of the skeptics who dismiss the whole thing as a fraud, remains a mystery. Was this "monster" merely a bad joke or is there some creature out there still waiting to be found?

AVIAN ANOMALIES

Pterosaurs in Palm Beach

In the summer of 1971 while stationed at Guantanamo Bay, Cuba on the other side of the Florida Straits, Eskin Cuhn claims to have seen two supposedly extinct avian animals. "I looked up and flying directly over me was a huge pterodactyl."

Cuhn claims that the animals were flying above him at a distance he estimates was no more than two hundred feet.

Additional sightings were reported in 1977. I myself responded to a sighting report in a then newly developed residential area of far western Palm Beach in 2002.

In the case I investigated in Palm Beach, I met with the two eyewitnesses at their home and enjoyed a particularly tasty long island ice tea with them while they related their account of the sighting.

Suddenly, there was a familiar sound in the skies above which, upon hearing it, my hosts turned quite pale. "There it is! I can't believe it showed up while you're here. That's the pterosaur. Do you hear it?"

My Northern legal beagle eyewitnesses who reported the "flying dinosaur" to me had never seen, nor heard, the Great Crested Sand Crane before.

Around the same time that my lawyer friends claimed to have seen and heard their "Pterosaur,: and not too far away, two guys were outside of a home in Jupiter, Florida talking to each other when a strange animal flew over their heads and into the backyard of the house.

A short time later, another of these animals flew in from a different direction and also landed in the rear of the home.

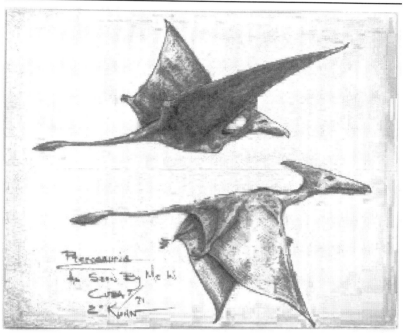

Eskin Cuhn's own drawing of the creature he saw flying over Guantanamo Bay in 1971.

According to their newspaper interview, the featherless "pterosaur" was a brownish beige and had a pointed beak. The animal, they claimed, had a rather long pointed crest jutting out from the back of its head. They also reported that the "flying lizard" had wingspan was about four feet and a pointed tail ending in a triangular flap of skin.

Their description is similar to that of a Rhamphorhynchus, a particular species of pterosaur that lived during the late Jurassic period. Its remains have been found in England, the Iberian Peninsula and in Central Africa. However the Rhamphorhynchus did not have a bony protrusion at the hack of its skull, although some other species of pterosaur and pterodactyl did.

Similar sightings with nearly identical descriptions are common in Central America and around the Southern Gulf of Mexico. Some sighting reports have even included video footage of the suspect creature in flight.

"Pterosaur" sightings of this type typically turn out to be a case of mistaken identity. Common animals like the pelican. In some cases, the Great Frigate Bird of Central America and the Galapagos Islands blown off-course are the most likely known animals to be mistaken for a pterodactyl.

However, there may be another explanation for at least some of the pterosaur sightings.

A Paleontologist at Texas Tech University, Sankar Chatterjee, and an aeronautical engineer, Rick Lind, of the University of Florida, along with their students, Andy Gedeon and Brian Roberts, are using the aerodynamics of the physical characteristics of a to develop what they call a "Pterodrone." The Pterodrone is an unmanned aircraft that can mimick the flight of a pterosaur. It can also imitate the way the animal walked and glided on thermals as did the living creature.

Chattergee and Lind revealed their work officially on October 7, 2008 at a neeting of the Geological Society of America in Houston, Texas.

Now, presumably, these two scientists have been testing their designs and, since the application of this stealth spy plane is military, it's likely that the testing ground has been remote areas of Elgin Air Force Base in the Panhandle or perhaps Avon Park Gunnery Range in Central Florida among other armed forces facilities here in the Sunshine State (and elsewhere).

While some sightings can be attributed to coincidence of the

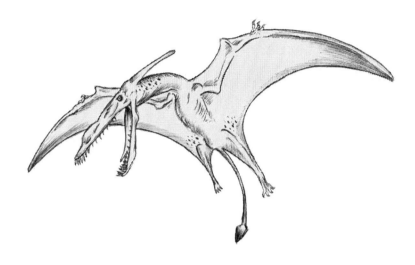

public seeing a cleaver deceptive contrivance like the Pterodrone, other sightings can not and remain up in the air, so to speak, as to whether there is a mechanical, biological or imaginary cause behind the sighting reports.

Thunderbirds

Thunderbirds – Giant condor-like avians — are occasionally reported over Florida. In the early 1990s, North of Tampa Bay, a youngster witnessed a "gigantic bird" while riding a school bus early one the morning.

I corresponded with the individual who saw the large avian several years later via email. He asserted that the animal had a wing span of around ten feet and that it was "definitely NOT a vulture," an animal with which he was very familiar.

The young man stated that the bird was mostly black with streaks of grey feathers beneath its wings and a white band around its neck — a description which is similar to that of an Andean condor.

However, the Andean condor has not been officially reported this far away from its normal habitat. I suppose that it could have been a California condor, but this possibility too is seems somewhat remote. Unless, of course, we're talking about an escapee from a local zoological park or animal rescue facility.

More recently, Don Davis saw a huge condor-like bird just west of northern Dade County outside of the Miami metropolis. He was working alone in a rock quarry getting in some weekend overtime.

Davis thought he saw a small plane in the distance coming toward him at an altitude of around 200 feet. Operating a large earth-moving machine with a 300 foot dragline, he was dumping a load of limestone material from the bucket when he noticed a "plane" flying rather low.

There were rows of material piles, about twenty piles in all,

between where he was working and this airborne object. The piles were more than one hundred feet high. "I would dump the material at the top of the end pile and could see this thing in the background. I would then swing away from the pile and dig another bucket of rock and again return to the top of the pile," he recalls.

Davis was able to see this flying: thing" getting closer with each load until it was only a few piles away from him. "The large window in front of me was wide open and I could hear no sound from a plane." Suddenly, it turned and did a full 180 in front of the boom and slightly above it. After completing the maneuver, the huge avian flapped its wings and then continued to glide towards the row of piles.

At this point, Davis knew that this was no airplane. "I stood there and watched until it was out of my sight. I have never seen or ever heard of any kind of bird of this great size."

Davis, as have many Floridians, had seen turkey vultures before and in insists that this "wasn't a buzzard," nor an eagle or large owl. It was "very large and was the size of an ultra light airplane or a Piper Cub."

When Davis later told a few friends about the sighting, they were understandably skeptical. They poked fun at him, so he kept the sighting to himself for about a year before finally reporting it to a cryptozoology friendly website. His encounter happened in 2008.

Some time before Davis' sighting, and in a highly publicized encounter in Illinois a seven year old boy, Marlon Lowe, was reportedly lifted off the ground by one avian monster bird. The event was witnessed by six adults.

Ancient North American Indian folklore speaks of giant "thunderbirds." The fossil record reveals that, at one time, the skies over Florida (and elsewhere in North America) were home to prehistoric teratorns — giant condor-like birds of prey — and many think that these ancient giant birds are the basis for the Native American legends — and contemporary sightings of "Thunderbirds."

Giant "Terror Birds" were, at one time, a menace to wildlife here as well. However, these birds were like the Ostrich and Emu and, regardless of their fearsome nature, could not fly.

Both of these giant birds are presumed to be extinct and are unlikely to be responsible for sightings of huge feathered creatures like those reported in these sighting accounts.

While it's more likely that a bird like the Turkey Vulture is the animal witnessed in these encounters, Turkey Vultures don't approach the size reported in these events. Even the giant condors of the Andes aren't large enough to carry off a human — despite the sensational scenes produced by Hollywood to this effect.

It's possible that the size estimates of these flying cryptids are in error because of a lack of reference when silhouetted against the sky. However bear in mind that, in the Davis case, he had the size of the machinery he was operating available to contrast to the giant bird he saw.

Could Thunderbirds — whatever they are — actually exist and still lurk undetected in the far reaches of Florida's back

TERRESTRIAL TERRORS

Hog Kong

Many people were enthralled with the wonderful National Geographic special on "Hogzilla" – a giant wild bovine shot in southern Georgia not far from the Florida state line and subsequently buried before being confirmed as a monster sized animal.

But few people know that a similar giant wild boar, a 1,140-pound Behemoth was killed by Larry Earley (see photo below) on his twenty-two acre farm near Leesburg, Florida in 2004.

You'll recall that Hogzilla was buried after it was taken and that its size and weight were exaggerated by the hunter according to National Geographic's special on the animal. However in the case of Hog Kong, Robert Bradow, the owner of Smokin' Oak Sausage Co. located in Branford, Florida measured and weighed the beast so that he could attest to Earley's monster hog before processing its meat.

Bradlow says, "That thing was unbelievably huge, the biggest hog I've ever seen. We've processed a lot of hogs and probably 450 pounds is the biggest we've ever handled before."

Earley relates that in late afternoon in August he Strolled on down to check on one of my dogs that was swimming in the pond" on his farm. The pond was frequented by a nine-foot alligator, so Early was concerned about the dog's safety.

"I was standing on the dock and saw the rear of this hog," he said. "At first I thought it was a cow that had gotten through my fence. Then I seen it from the side and made out an eight-inch tusk."

Earley, an avid hog hunter, ran back to his house and got his 44 Smith & Wesson handgun. By the time Earley got back, the giant hog had moved and was rooting by the edge of the pond where his dogs had taken refuge from the beast.

Earley circled stealthfuly so he could get a side shot and crept up to the animal. When he was about ten yards away from the animal he fired one round.

"(The hog) grunted real hard and turned and started coming at me," Earley later related. "I backed up and tried to keep a bead on him, but he made about three jumps and fell over sideways a couple of feet from me."

Earley had had experience previously with a hog weighing two hundred and thirty pounds but knew this one was much bigger. He estimated that it would come in at four hundred to five hundred pounds. Among hog hunter, a three hundred pound boar is considered a giant, but a four hundred pound wild hog is nothing short of a nightmare.

There wasn't a large enough scale on his farm, so Earley and some friends loaded "Hog Kong" onto a flatbed he used for hauling cars. Earley then took off up I-75 to the Suwannee River Ranch near Branford. The Suwannee River Ranch is a hunting preserve owned by Earley's boyhood friend, John

Kruzeski. The preserve has a half-ton game scale.

Kruzeski said, "'Man, that thing weighs 1,000 pounds," and knew an even bigger scale would be needed. That's when Bradow was called in.

"There was over three hundred pounds of boneless meat," Kruzeski said. "We have a rule of thumb, the thirds rule — one-third for the head and hide, one-third for the internal viscera, one-third for the carcass. My math told me we were looking at a 1,140 to 1,200 pound beast."

Comparisons of "Hog Kong" to the more publicized "Hogzilla" aren't confirmed. But "Hogzilla's" weight is estimated at 1,000 pounds and it measured twelve feet in length and had nine-inch tusks.

Monstrous hogs indeed!

Okeechobee Serpent

Giant snakes are another frequently reported cryptid – some have been said to measure over thirty feet long.

Now it's well know that exotic snake species are wrecking havoc among Florida's native wildlife population. Most reports involve exotic pets that were illegally released and went feral. One hundred and ninety seven Boa Constructors were taken out of the Florida Everglades last year alone.

A favorite Internet chat room and forum staple a couple of years ago was the photo of a giant python that took on a six-foot alligator –- the alligator lost.

After ingesting the 'gator, the snake was also attacked by another crocodilian which caused it to burst open when punctured by the gator's teeth.

But, few people today know that unusually giant snakes have been reported here in Florida for a very long time. We've already discussed the Lake Clinch serpent beast.

For over a hundred years giant snakes have been a tradition among the Seminole Indians on the Brighton Indian Reservation which borders Lake Okeechobee. Before the 20th Century, the Indians there told of an immense serpent which made its home in the Everglades and had carried off at least two villagers there.

In a 1901 newspaper article. Buster Farrell, a noted hunter in the Okeechobee vicinity, who was a twenty year resident of the lake and the Everglades, killed an immense serpent there.

While making one of his regular treks into the wilds, Farrell noted what appeared at first to be the game trail of a gigantic alligator. Returning to the area frequently for a while, Farrel intended to kill the 'gator but he was unsuccessful in locating it. So Farrell used a large cypress tree near the game trail and set up a tree stand in which he waited for the beast to show.

Farrel remained on watch, with his rifle at the ready, for two days without seeing the animal. But, on the third day, before he had been on his stand for an hour, Farrell was awestruck by a huge snake slithering along the alligator game trail.

From the safety of his perch, Farrell estimated the serpent to be about twenty to thirty feet in length and at least ten to twelve inches across where the head met the rest of its body. He said that it was "as large around as a rain barrel ten feet farther back along its length."

Apparently sensing danger, the snake stopped and raised its bead to take a precautionary look around. Within the range of his rifle, Farrell opened fire on it aiming at its head.

The snake fled into the swamp at an amazing speed, as Farrell repeatedly fired at. Although apparently hit several times, Farrell's shots failed to stop it.

Less than a week later, Farrell went back into the area to check things out again. About a mile from where Farrel had his frightening encounter with the snake, a large flock of vultures were feasting on the remains of the creature.

The buzzards had mangled the body and head so badly that Farrell couldn't save the animal's skin. Nevertheless, Farrell saved the monster's head which measured ten inches from jaw to jaw. The mouth contained a considerable number of razor-like teeth.

A period illustration from a photograph of South American hunters and their giant snake kill.

Period descriptions of the creature state that it was dark in color on its back with dingy white on its belly below. An odd characteristic that was reported was that the animal had feelers around its mouth like those of a catfish.

According to a newspaper account in the New York Times, Farrell later ventured back into the swamp intending to recover the skeleton of the beast and send it to the Smithsonian Institution In Washington, DC.

Following up on this lead I got in touch with Jeremy F Jacobs, Collections Manager Amphibians and Reptiles, at the Smithsonian to see if any remains had been submitted to them by Farrell.

Museums typically catalog or collectibles than the catalog entry usually includes a description of the item, the date received, the name of a contributor and other information pertinent to the specimen.

Jacobs conducted a quick check of the museum's collections

database while he was on the phone with me . His query did not turn up any specimen sent to the museum by a "Buster Farrell."

But Farrell himself was a real character. According to "History of Okeechobee County " by Kyle S. Van Landingham and Alma Hetherington, W. A. "Buster" Farrell settled there around 1898 and built a house a short distance west of Taylor Creek. Farrell's reputation as a hunter preceded him.. However he became an orchard grower and planted an orange grove around his home. Farrell is also remembered as the first commercial fishermen in the Taylor Creek vicinity.

The fact that Farrell apparently did not follow through with the claim made by the New York Times in submitting his monster snake to the Smithsonian does not necessarily discount the events related in the article (despite the minor misspelling of Farrell's last name in the article).

We've already seen that giant serpents living near or in large bodies of water here in Florida may have been relatively common in the end before the early 20th century based on Native American legends and stories like that of Charles Mercer Mallett. It may simply have been a matter of Farrell's inability to retrieve viable remains that are the reason behind his failure to send the specimen to the museum.

While the giant snakes plague Florida today are not the gargantuan beasts that apparently inhabited the state during its pioneer days, there is little question that giant exotic reptiles are still found here.

Black Panthers

Among the more frequently reported cryptids found in Florida are "Black Panthers." I myself have seen one of these melanistic big cats just inside the front gate of the Oscar Shearer State Park down near Venice, Florida two years ago.

It was early in the morning and two of my sons and I broke camp early to head back home for a morning appointment. The boys were asleep in the bunk of the RV and I was driving out at seven in the morning shortly after daybreak.

A Florida Panther Track found in the Big Cypress Swamp of Southwest Florida

The "Experts" tell me that Florida Panthers can't be melanistic. I beg to differ with them. I've had the pleasure of helping raise and care for Florida panthers. I know what they look like, their profile, normal colorations from birth to adulthood, how they walk and so forth. What I saw was a Florida Panther and it was black.

The term "Melanistic" comes from "melanin" — a chemical which gives skin and hair a dark color. With cats, melanism causes the animal's fur to appear very dark or black in color. Similar to that of the black jaguar of Central America. Sometimes underlying markings can be seen faintly through fur coat when seen at certain angles or in bright sunlight. Melanistic cats are usually born to litters of mixed colorations that include normally colored siblings.

Since there are no documented cases of melanistic cougars, the cat family to which Florida Panthers belong, it is widely accepted among biologists and handlers that the condition is not possible for this species.

However, black cougars are regularly reported in the Southeastern United States from Kentucky to the Carolinas and south into Florida. There are also reports of black cougars in Kansas, Texas and Nebraska.

Moreover, black cougars feature prominently in Choctaw folklore where, along with the owl, these cats usually portend death.

Most of the time, sightings of "Black Panthers" are dismissed by experts as a mistake in species identification by lay people unfamiliar with native fauna or by exaggeration of the animal's size. This is probably true in some sighting reports.

Melanistic bobcats have been captured in Florida and these cats, although much smaller, have probably been mistaken for panthers.

Adult male bobcats are twenty-eight to forty-seven inches in length and they have a short, bobbed tail. Bobcats stand eighteen to twenty-four inches tall at the shoulder. Bobcats weigh sixteen to thirty pounds. As with most mammals, female bobcats are a bit more slight in their size.

Florida panthers are five to seven feet long (this includes the tail) and twenty-three to thirty-two inches tall at the shoulder. The tail is long. Florida panthers weigh in at fifty to one hundred and fifty pounds, again depending on gender.

So, as you can see, people who are familiar with these so-called "big cats" are not likely to confuse these two species.

I've mentioned the black jaguar. At one time, these cats

ranged into North America and were hunted to near-extinction in the 1960s. It's presumed that these animals retreated south into Central America where they are rare, but still seen from time to time in the wild.

However, to the discerning eye jaguars, black or tan, while similar in size, don't look exactly like cougars or our Florida Panther. But the Black jaguar has been reported and photographed in Arizona, New Mexico, Oklahoma, and Southwest Texas.

So, assuming that this large cat, like the coyote, has managed to migrate to Florida from these regions, it's possible that it could be responsible for at least some "Black Panther" sightings here.

The Elusive Jaguarundi

Some people suggest that the Jaguarundi is also a possible explanation for Black Panther sightings in Florida and elsewhere in the United States.

The Jaguarundi is a diurnal feral feline which is a bit bigger in size than a domestic cat, but smaller than a bobcat. Their fur can be either a reddish-brown or a dark grey-black. Their legs are shorter than a domestic cat and they have a long, bushy tail. This causes them to run in an undulating manner giving rise to their popular nickname "The Otter Cat."

These exotic cats are known animals in South and Central America. However, there have been confirmed sighting reports of them in southern Texas, Arizona and New Mexico.

In South and Central America, they are kept as popular pets. As far as non-domesticated animals go. In the wild, a male jaguarondi's range is up to forty square miles. The female's home range can be up to eight square miles.

Susan Bogue. A student of Professor Roland Fisch at the Florida Keys Community College writes:

Panthers in the keys have always been a mystery to me as my older relatives accounts of panthers often included black panthers at my Uncles house in the 40s. The house has long since demolished, but it was on the Port Bouganvillea/Dagney Johnson State Park property.

Whenever I researched this possiblility, they mentioned no black mutations of the panther. I even asked several years ago in one of your classes "Were there black panthers here." Out of context it must've seemed an easy yes or no question to which you explained something about color and theories on the panthers and mutations but essentially you answered, "No."

But when you spoke of the jaguarundi in this class the pieces fell together as THAT was quite possibly what my relatives were describing. So I emailed my mom and got her account in writing I did not mention the jaguarundi and just asked my mom to write out her memories of the black panthers in the Keys.

The "uncle Johnny" she speaks of was a rum runner with my grandfather during prohibition. My great grandfather worked on the railroad and lived in Key West, but my grandparents decided to live the more glamorous Key Biscayne. They participated

The remains of an unfortunate jaguarundi killed by a car in High-lands County, Florida. The photograph appeared in "Florida Wild-life" in 1961.

in the life and adventure of the Hemingway style in the Keys on weekends and vacations at the various fishing houses the family owned here. I met Unlce Johnny, who wore a fake nose on his sunglasses after the sun ate his nose off all those years ago

This is what Susan's mother had to say:

Now concerning the panthers on the keys. This would have been in the early to late 40's.

We used to go down to Uncle Johnny's on a regular basis. There were two things that he was insistent about, mostly getting in by dark:

The mosquitoes were terrible, they would litterally swarm in a black cloud. You could see them coming. I can remember him standing at the top of those tall stairs, and waving a big white rag, towel or the like, hollering, "Get in here quick!" Move fast! Don't let the skitters in"

The panthers often would come up quite close to the house. We would often hear them crying nearby. I actually only saw one once, and just caught a quick look. I was just a small child. What I remember was that it looked black, was not real large, like you think of as a cougar. Imagine a very LARGE back cat. The tail was very long, and the head seemed bigger definitely not a regular domestic cat.

There were reports of people seeing them quite frequently, and there was definite evidence of their presence.

My uncle often told of them getting into the chickens, or other livestock that people had at the time. Others that we knew told similar stories. I did however see their footprints below the house quite a few times over the years that went to his house.

My Mom would become quite frightened when we would hear them crying, and would refuse to sleep on a screened in porch. (Screened? I Wonder why?) I remember sleeping with my parents several times, because of being scared.

After my parents got their little lot there on Plant Street, the area which would be north of the house, there on the Keys was all woods. I vaguely remember sometimes hearing something that sounded like that unique sound. Daddy said that it was probably a panther. That would have been very early, like 1950-51. At that time we were one of just a few houses. There was probably maybe 2-3 houses In the whole subdivision and they were quite far apart. One was way up on the highway, Old US 1 which was only a small narrow two lane road, with very little influence by people on either side.

Therefore it would have been possible for the panthers to have been in the area. At one time I vaguely remember someone had a picture of a panther that had been killed. I don't know if Eddie would have access to those old pictures, or maybe they belonged to another older relative.

There were so many things of that time period that were special but as a child, I didn't realize the significance or importance of them. It just seemed rather the norm for me. I never thought anything about the fact that we had an icebox and they brought ice to it or that we drew water from a well in Miami, or a Cistern down there in the Keys.

As you see, being significantly smaller than a Florida Panther and quite different in overall appearance with their low to the ground build and unusual feline movement, or standout characteristics for this cat. Susan's mother observed, people may call the Jaguarundi a "Black Panther" but anyone other than a total wildlife greenhorn would be able to discern the difference between it and the real thing.

Previously thought to be a member of the puma family, and then the Felis genus, the animal is now classified as Herpailurus yaguarondi to science.

Susan's mother also mentions Jasguarundi road kill. Indeed there have been some traffic mishaps involving the cat and photos of them have appeared in newspapers after these accidents. However, the remains of the animal were apparently not kept that have been discarded.

We at Pangea Institute have something of a debate going on with regard to this known animal found outside of its natural habitat.

Dr. Edward Petuch believes that the animal has been here in Florida since the Pleistocene Era and the secretive cat has gone undetected as a sub-species of the Herpalaria genus.

My associate, Lisa Wojcik thinks that the Jaguarondi was bought here during the 1940s and released by a well-meaning — but misguided — naturalist named Verrill.

My personal take is that the animal migrated here along the Gulf Coast from Mexico as have Coyote and other animals indigenous to the Southwestern United States.

Pangea is currently engaged in ongoing expeditions designed to capture one of these creatures to perform the DNA test necessary to discover which of us is right.

Mainstream wildlife biologists are loath to accept Jaguarundi sighting reports here in Florida despite the fact that there have been several road kill incidents, some with supporting photography, involving the animal.

The rejection typically hinges on the animals daylight hunting characteristics. They reason that a diurnal animal would have been seen and recognized by now. But in fact they have been. I've spoken to a number of Rangers in the Everglades, shark Valley, and Merritt Island who have seen the animal. Ranchers and other laypeople have also had sightings and accurately described it.

One reason that there haven't been a greater number of reports is that this animal is proficient at concealing its identity because it often can pass as a domestic house cat. As a result people who see it, and aren't looking for it, simply overlook it.

The Carrabelle Cat Mystery

On April 2, 2010 the following story appeared in the Apalachicola Times newspaper:

CARRABELLE - Some unusual wildlife has been reported in Tate's Hell recently. Could there be big cats haunting the swamp?

If you view this YouTube video (see www.youtube.com/watch?v=jUDE8b6Zsgk), be prepared to see something unusual. What appears to be a big black cat slinks toward the camera and then turns and stalks off into the underbrush.

FRAME TAKEN FROM VIDEO

Larry Miller of Carrabelle was hunting in a deer blind off Mill Road in Carrabelle when he captured the Carrabelle Cat on tape.

Miller said, "I saw it four days in a row. On the fourth day, I took my wife to the blind. As we walked in, we heard it growling at us in the bushes. It was in the tall grass when we walked out and I showed it to my wife."

Miller said he believed the cat weighed about 30-40 pounds.

"It was definitely bigger than a housecat, but not as big as a panther," he said. "It might attack a house pet but not a human. It wasn't big enough to take even a small deer."

The sightings occurred late in the afternoon. Miller said he believed the animal was hunting birds. He said it looked healthy and well fed with glossy coal black fur, bright yellow eyes and pointed ears.

He said he has seen Florida panthers both caged and in the wild and the cat he saw was not a panther.

"I was curious, not scared and I walked toward it and it turned tail and ran," he said.

Miller said one of his customers who lives on Mill Road volunteered that he had seen a very similar animal sunning on his boardwalk some weeks earlier.

In a telephone interview, another Carrabelle resident said he glimpsed a 4 foot long black cat with a long tail leap across the road in broad daylight near Larry Drive in Carrabelle.

"I've seen bobcats come through my yard," he said. "This was bigger."

Bruce McKinnon, volunteer manager of the Womack Creek Campground in the Apalachicola State Forest said he has seen dark brown cats with long tails that appeared to weigh around 50 pounds in the forest on three occasions. He said he once saw a cat ran across River Road followed shortly by a bear and then by a second cat.

McKinnon said he very rarely sees domestic cats in the state forest.

Miller said he first heard rumors of a big cat in the swamp from Cal Allen of Carrabelle.

Cal Allen, who said he has seen large felines on several occasions wrote, "On my way up Highway 67, 17 miles by odometer from Highway 98 (in the Hitchcock lake area), I was on my way to the Bear Creek Feline Center, last Friday (March 19) when a black cat that looked exactly like the one in Larry's video stepped out into the oncoming lane and at the center line turned and walked back into the woods when it saw me. I was about 150 yards from it when it went back into the bushes. And, my long distance vision is excellent. This was about 20 miles from Larry's site."

In Sept. 2009, he saw what he first thought was a black guardrail off CR 67. This too was actually a large cat.

On a third occasion earlier this year, Allen said he saw a pair of yellow orange cats about 75 yards ahead of him on Dry Bridge Road north of US 98. He described all 4 cats as 60 to 70 pounds with long tales. All were observed during the day.

Allen also has what he believes are droppings of the elusive cat and has found a pair of indentations in the sand he believes the cat created. He also found tracks but so far has been unsuccessful in creating a plaster cast of most of them. One set that he was able to lift were identified as coyote tracks.

He remains convinced that there is an unknown feline or felines loose in the woods around Carrabelle and is on a mission to prove he is right.

A jaguarundi maybe?

Allen said the animals might be jaguarundis, a rare cat native to South America but also found in southern Texas and Arizona. The cats are also known as weasel cats, otter cats and catamounts. A close relative of pumas, jaguarundis are about the size of a large house cat. They are similar to an otter in appearance with distinctive short legs and rounded ears. They may be dark brown, yellow or dark grey.

Jaguarundis eat mostly birds but also consume fish and are good swimmers. Unlike many wild felines, jaguarundis are active during the day.

Rumors have long circulated that there are jaguarundis in Florida but no physical evidence, documented film footage or photograph of a Florida jaguarundi exists and they are not found in Florida's fossil record.

Gathana Parmenas of Carrabelle believes she encountered a jaguarundi at the cement bridge near Victorian Village on US 98 west of Carrabelle.

"It was going down to the water," she said, "which is jaguarundi-like behavior. It was a cat of a type that I've never seen with the long neck and the slinky motion when it moved. I've had lots of house cats I know what they look like. It wasn't an otter. It was definitely a cat and definitely not a house cat. When I looked on the Internet, I decided it was a jaguarundi."

Could the Carrabelle Cat be a bobcat?

In 1941, the Journal of Mammalogy published pictures of two black bobcats killed in Marion County Florida. Those bobcats were mistaken for panthers by casual observers at the time.

In 2007, a south Florida woman called authorities after a "black panther" ate her pet turkey. The panther was actually a 20 pound melanistic bobcat which now resides at the Busch Wildlife Sanctuary in Jupiter, Florida.

David Hitzig curator of the sanctuary captured the cat. He said before the cat was captured, the woman insisted the animal weighed 100 pounds and would not fit in the trap he brought to the scene.

Bobcats weigh about 20 pounds and have short stumpy tails.

The animal in Miller's video is certainly not a bobcat since a long tail is clearly visible.

Could the Carrabelle Cat be a panther?

Tate's Hell was once home to Florida panthers, also known as the eastern puma. According to local legend, a farmer pursued a panther that was killing his livestock into the swamp. He got lost and remained in the wilderness for ten days, before stumbling into a clearing near Carrabelle, where he died. His final words were "My name is Cebe Tate and I have been to hell." Thus the region got it's name.

In an article reprinted in the Times on January 14, the late Charles Marks wrote that there were pumas on St. Vincent Island when he grew up there during the 1920s.

There are still sporadic reports of cat tracks on the beach at Indian Pass.

Michael Allen of Eastpoint, who is unrelated to Cal Allen, said he saw a yellow cat weighing 80 to 100 pounds cross U.S. 65 in the early 1990s. He said he, initially, believed that it was an escaped zoo or circus animal until he discussed the sighting with Woody Miley former director of the Apalachicola National Estuarine Research Reserve. Miley told him the cat was probably a puma.

Darrell Land, Panther Team Leader for Florida Fish and Wildlife, said 20 Texas pumas were released in north Florida during the 1990s as part of an experiment to see if Florida panthers could survive here. Michael Allen's cat could have been one of these. He said that the panthers released for the experiment were able to survive but several were killed by vehicles. At the end of the study, the remaining cats were trapped and removed. Michael Allen's panther could have been one of these.

Land said that, at any given time, there are also 15 to 20 male panthers wandering north of Lake Ocala. These are young males displaced during territory conflicts with older males.

The late Jay MacDonald, the former Womack Creek campground manager, said he saw a Florida panther walk through the campground in a 2008 interview.

Parmenas said she too saw a puma in 2003 about 6 miles north of Carrabelle on CR 67 just at dusk.

Myron and Ellen Stitt visit Franklin County annually from their home near Delaware Ohio. Last February, they encountered a Florida panther in Tate's Hell. Myron said, "We like your back woods and we were driving in Tate's Hell heading south on Tower Road just two miles south of State Road 65. It was February and we had just arrived. We saw a tawny yellow cat just at dusk. It was going from west to east when it crossed the road."

Male Florida panthers may range hundreds of miles. A Florida panther was shot by a hunter in Georgia in 2008. The Louisiana Department of Fisheries and Wildlife receives reports of pumas every year, most of which remain unconfirmed. Both Louisiana and Georgia were in the Florida panther's original range.

The cat in Miller's video cannot be a puma. Pumas are blondes. Scientists say a black puma has never been observed.

Land said that, when large black cats occur, it is normally a dark form of leopard or jaguar. Black cats are actually spotted cats where the spotting is very dense.

Miller and McKinnon both insist the animal they saw in Tate's Hell could not be a Florida panther.

Jim Broaddus, owner of the Bear Creek Feline Center, a refuge and educational center for big cats in Panama City said Miller's video does not appear to be either a panther or a jaguarundi.

The search for 'Little Foot'

Broaddus said that he and other cat enthusiasts are involved in a project to document the existence of jaguarundis in Florida.

"We call it the search for 'Little Foot,'" he said, "Florida Fish and Wildlife Conservation Commission (FWC) gave us the nod to capture a jaguarundi because they don't exist."

He said he would especially like to capture a female jaguarundi to breed with a captive male already living in his compound.

Broaddus said that interns, who volunteer at his facility and are familiar with big cats, frequently see panthers when they leave and go home.

He suggested that camera traps with motion sensors could be used to photograph the Carrabelle Cat. He said they are available on-line for around $100. He advised anyone attempting to catch the cat on film to mount the camera in an area where the animal has been spotted and leave it for several days. He said high quality paw prints might be captured by smoothing out the sand under the camera mount.

Broaddus believes the animal could be some kind of a hybrid between a domestic cat and a wild cat. He said that hybrid females are often fertile.

A number of wild cat species have been interbred with domestic cats.

Craig Mariconi owner of the Wild Spots Cattery in Benton, Arkansas, breeds Cheetoh cats, a hybrid variety with lineage from the Asian Leopard Cat. He does not breed wild cats with domestic animals but has experience in the process. He said that hybridization can occur but it is rare.

"The different species have different gestation periods," he said. This means that hybrid kittens are rarely carried to full term and most do not survive.

Adam Warwick, a wildlife biologist and bear specialist for the FWC said he has viewed the Miller video with other wildlife specialists. He said they have come to the conclusion that the animal is a large housecat.

He said none of his FWC colleagues in Franklin County or neighboring areas has seen any unknown cat.

"As much as we are in the woods, you would think one of us would have seen something," he said. "Nothing would make me happier than to think there *was a healthy population of panthers in Tate's Hell. I haven't seen any hard evidence of any unknown animal and I've run it by several people who have more experience than I do."*

He said that coyote tracks are frequently confused with cat tracks.

He added that he does not dismiss sightings of Florida jaguarundis out of hand.

"I've heard some things that make me wonder," he said.

Land and Hitzig concur with Warwick on the identity of the YouTube Cat.

Land said, "It's a house cat. The animal is pictured on a road and it doesn't even stretch across a single tire track. A panther would have easily stretched between two ruts. They're that big."

FWC Wildlife biologist Mark Lotz, who specializes in panthers, said there is no evidence to refute the existence of the large cats people say they have seen but there is no evidence to support the existence of the cats either.

He said, "One of the interesting things about sightings of rare animals is that they can usually be reproduced if the animal is genuine. Somebody can go back and spot the animal again. There are no native black cats in North America. Bobcats have a melanistic phase, but it's extremely rare. Sometimes, when you glimpse something, your mind fills in the gaps. It's easy to convince yourself you saw something."

Lotz concurs that the cat in the YouTube video is a house cat.

Cal Allen is convinced that the YouTube cat is much larger than a normal house cat. He described it as a "cat on steroids" setting the length at 28.9 inches after some complicated mathematics. He sets the rear end height at 20 inches. Tail length with some extrapolating would be 18-19 inches.

He wrote, "It seems too big for a jaguarundi, and too small and wrong color for a panther. Hybrid? Maybe, but of what? Plus, that wouldn't explain multiple sightings of what the locals call "Black Panther" that I have heard from several other people."

If you see the Carrabelle Cat, do not attempt to approach it and do not shoot at it or harm it in any way. All native big cats are protected in the US.

The story was filed by Dr. Lois Swoboda who has since become my friend over the course of my investigation into this mystery cat. Her story makes a good starting point for this case because it covers the essential facts and introduces the "players" who later come into focus.

But, perhaps I'm getting ahead of myself.

Shortly after Lois' story appeared, I was contacted by city council member, Cal Allen, who was mentioned in the newspaper account. Cal met with me on a trip down to Tampa to discuss the strange cryptid and to enlist my aid in identifying the odd feline.

I agreed to check it out and shortly thereafter made a trip up to the Panhandle where Cal arranged for me to meet up with the Hunter, Larry Miller, who shot the video of the animal (which he had posted to YouTube) that had caused such a stir in cryptozoology circles.

Larry took Cal, my son Robert and myself to the spot where he had signted and filmed the cat just several month before. I gathered details and took a few measurements as well as surveyed the area to get a feel for the wildlife found there. The location is on private land owned by the local gas company off River Road adjacent to the Tate's Hell State Forest.

After a lengthy interview with Larry and additional discussion with Cal, I obtained the actual video footage shot by Miller and took the film back to my home to review.

I reviewed the film and extracted several frames from the video that I enlarged and enhanced to get a better look at the mystery cat.

Miller and Allen were both adamant that the animal was a jaguarundi. However, I wasn't so sure. From Larry's description of the animal's size and the movements it made in the video, I ruled out the jaguarundi in favor of a juvenile Florida Panther at first. But, I wasn't entirely sure of that determination either.

When I got to the frame of the video that's pictured above, I knew for certain that the cat wasn't a jaguarundi. The jaguarundi don't have the pointed ears normally seen on a typical cat and the jaguarundi's legs are considerably shorter than the cat in the image.

However, the feline's profile also didn't fit that of a Florida Panther -- juvenile or otherwise. So I was dubious of that animal being the "culprit" feline.

Comparing the silhouette of the cat in the image above to known felines that I thought could explain the Carrabelle Cat, I ruled out a Bobcat (tail isn't short nor is the profile as robust), Jaguar (head shape is not right nor is the video cat as large) and Florida Panther (the legs are too massive on the Panther compared to those of the video cat).

That left the obvious solution of a common house cat and the South American Geoffroy's Cat. But, Miller insisted that the cat he saw was "not a housecat."

Taking Larry at his word, I privately settled on the Geoffroy's Cat as the most likely "critter."

In the meantime, Cal Allen called me to report that he'd found several tracks -- apparently made by the mystery cat -- in the sandy roadway of one of the access roads inside the Tate's Hell State Forest preserve.

Cal emailed the photo to me. His photo appears on the next page (lower right) in the comparison with those of the other suspect cats (except that of a Geoffroy's Cat which I do not

SILHOUETTES OF SUSPECT FELINES

House Cat   Jaguarundi

Geoffroy's Cat   Bobcat

Florida Panther   Jaguar

have in my image file).

I didn't see any similarity between Carrabrelle Cal's foot print with any of the felines I was able to compare it to at the time. Thus, I had no reason to discount my belief that the mystery cat was an escaped exotic species -- I.E. the Geoffroy's Cat -- that had somehow found its way to the Carrabelle area. Moreover, I felt that the black mystery cat was easily explained by the Geoffroy's Cat in as much as the Geoffroy's species was known to have a melanistic variant.

So, I planned on making another trip up to the Panhandle to deliver my findings and put the case to rest. However,

COMPARISON OF CAT TRACKS WITH RE-PORTED CARABELLE CAT PRINT

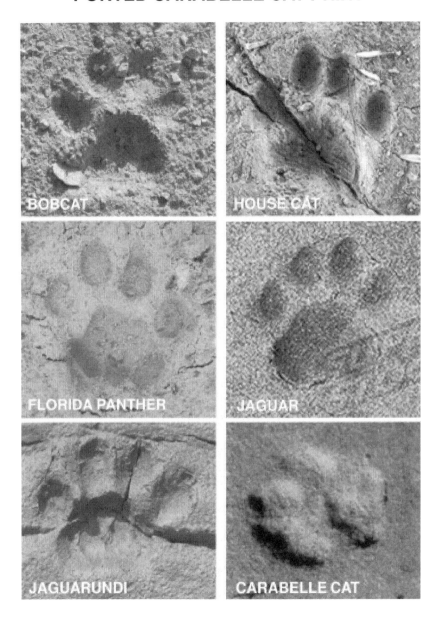

Here are two Geoffroy Cat's. The one on the right is normally colored. The one on the left is a melanstic phase.

circumstances unraveled differently than I had anticipated.

On meeting with Cal I was introduced to Jim Broaddus (also mentioned in Lois Swaboda's story who ran the Bear Creek Feline Center in Panama City, Florida. In describing his facility to me, Jim mentioned that the animals in his care included all of the suspect species of feline that I had considered as candidates for the Carrabelle Cat -- with the exception of the Jaguar which I had ruled out anyway.

Now, I began to wonder if the signting events were some sort of ruse designed to foster some interest in Florida's Forgotten Coast by cryptozoology buffs, biologists and naturalists in the hope that the story would generate some eco-tourism interest in the area.

So, I decided not to announce my findings at that time and

laid low. The reader will recall that I had similar experiences with the Lake Worth Monster and the Muck Monster down in Palm Beach. Thus, I reasoned that the truth of the matter would be revealed given enough time for a deliberate hoax to unravel.

At that point, I got in touch with my friend and Colleague, Ken Gerhard, in Texas and spoke to him about organizing an expedition to conduct a bit more research into the Mystery Cat. Ken, in turn, contacted wildlife biologist, Lee Hales who has appeared with me on the Piranhas episode of MonsterQuest.

The three of us were able to work out a schedule and agreed to meet up in the Carrabelle area for a 4 day expedition camping out at the Ochlockonee River State Park located a little north of Carrabelle on Route 319.

However, it would be several months before we could all clear our schedules to make time for our exploration of the Carrabelle Cat Mystery.

In the meantime, I had been stopping by the Manatee Springs and Fanning Springs State Parks to check up on any signting reports arising from my previous research work with colleague Lisa Wojcik (See the chapter on "The Elusive Jaguarundi" in this book) on the way up to Carrabelle to look into their Mystery Cat.

On one such drop in visit, one of the rangers at Fanning Springs handed me the photo appearing on th next page. The picture was taken at the park by a member of the park staff with a trap camera. Clearly, this cat was not a housecat and much bigger than the animal seen in Larry Miller's video. The feline's profile is a match to that of a Florida Panther, however, the cat is most obviously melanistic -- something

that most wildlife biologists assert is not possible.

At about the same time, I received two emails from Jim Broaddus:

08/07/2011

Get this: On the way to the tribal council meeting yesterday, we traveled East on Hwy 267 through the Apalachicola National Forest. At 2:15 PM central time, with Bertie (Jim's wife) driving, she applied her breaks when we both spotted an animal about 600 feet in front of us meandering across the road. It was almost as wide as one traffic lane from nose to tip of tail. The tail was easily as long as the body. As we neared the animal, we positively conclude that we saw an adult, melanistic panther! I know a panther when I see one; this cat was black as the ace of spades, moving with a typical panther gate, then bounding of the highway into the bush when we were about 200 feet away. Although I had the movie camera with me, it was in a bag in the rear of the SAAB. I recorded the approximate location of this sighting, and I will be going back to look for tracks on the slim chance of further documenting this sighting.

Best,
Jim

And again . . .

08/08/2011

Scott: More on the black panther sighting. We have submitted our sighting to the FFWCC. They say that the black panther does not live in the Florida wilds, but know, I know better.

We had been traveling East on Hwy 267 for about 10 miles after turning off Hwy 20, West of Tallahassee, in the Apalachicola National Forest. If you Google this area, the cat was seen between the Hwy 20/267 intersection and the intersection of Hwy 267/319. The closest land mark is Wakulla Springs State Park. This sighting was not near any town....maybe 60 miles from Tallahassee and even further away from BCFC.

I always politely tell those who report melanistic panther sighting that they probably saw a tawny beige panther in either early morning or late afternoon sunlight, when they appear to be black at a distance. Our sighting was at 2:15 PM in the bright Sunlight at approximately 200 feet! Make no mistake, this was a melanistic puma concolor, not a leopard or a jaguar. I am 100 % positive. The sighting began at about 600 feet and ended at maybe 200 feet. Lets say maybe +/- 10 seconds total. Long enough for me to make positive identification. I do not drink and my far sighted vision is nearly perfect. Bertie saw the cat before I did, as she was driving at the time of this sighting, with both eyes on the road.

BTW.....on the way back from Perry, we saw a wild hog and two deer in the same vicinity, so this big cat had plenty of prey from which to choose. This cat was well fed and seemed very confident as he strolled across the highway. I feel extremely lucky to have had this experienced and I am most humbled by it!

Best,
Jim

When I first had met Jim, I sported the idea that the Carrabelle Cat could be a melanistic Florida Panther -- as i had seen one before at Oscar Shearer State Park -- just to see how he would respond. Both Jim and his friend Jim Thornton formerly of Mutual of Omaha's "Wild Kingdom," poo-pooed the idea and found it laughable since near every wildlife biologist and naturalist considers it impossible for a Puma concolor to be of black coloration because none in captivity has ever been born as such nor has any of them been captured with melanistic traits.

Now, here was Jim having had a sighting of a Black Florida Panther himself. And, of course, Jim cares for several Panthers at his facility. So he knows exactly what he was seeing. Was this assertion fact -- in the light of the Fanning Springs sighting -- or just a little too convenient?

I was intrigued . . .

WILBURN "CURLEY" MESSER
MAYOR/COMMISSIONER

FRANKLIN MATHES
COMMISSIONER

JAMES N. BROWN
COMMISSIONER

CHAROLETTE SCHNEIDER
COMMISSIONER

CAL ALLEN
COMMISSIONER

CITY OF CARRABELLE
CARRABELLE, FLORIDA

DAN HARTMAN
CITY ATTORNEY

COURTNEY DEMPSEY
CITY ADMINISTRATOR

KEISHA SMITH
CITY CLERK

1001 GRAY AVENUE
CARRABELLE, FLORIDA 52322
TELEPHONE: 850-697-36XX
FAX: 850-697-3196

Dr. Scott Marlowe
Pangea Institute
514 Winter Terrace
Winter Haven, Florida 33881

Dear Dr. Marlowe,

Thank you so much for your interest in an unidentified big black cat that has become known locally as the "Carrabelle Cat." In addition to a video taken by a local hunter, there have been numerous sightings, in the area known as "Tate's Hell State Forest," near Carrabelle.

Please consider this letter as an invitation from our City Commission to bring an your expedition here to help identify this beautiful animal. We understand the tentative dates to be March 2-4 of 2012.

We wish for you and the institute the best success in your quest.

Regards,

Courtney Dempsey
City Administrator

Cal Allen had been informed that Ken, Lee and I would be making a trip to Carrabelle to conduct more research into the Mystery Cat. Cal took our plans to the city council and shortly thereafter, I received an official request from the City of Carrabelle (see letter reproduced above) requesting that my team investigate the matter. As far as I know, this was the first time any avowed cryptozoologist was ever asked to investigate a case like this by a governmental authority.

Of course, I keep my colleagues up to date on events as they occurred and the date finally came for us to meet up for the expedition.

Mother nature, unfortunately, had other ideas. It rained for 3 of the 4 days we had set aside for the research severely limiting the work we could perform. But, Ken and Lee being the professionals they are weathered the storms and did what investigation could be accomplished -- beginning with retracing my steps by interviewing Larry Miller and Cal Allen and visiting the site where the cat was filmed.

By this time, I had privately concluded that the Mystery Cat was actually several cats of different species that the local residents had been encountering. But, I kept this belief to myself in the hope that my colleagues would either arrive at the same conclusion themselves or would come up with some entirely different theory that explained the sighting reports.

While we were all out at the location of the original sighting, earnestly searching for the cat, Larry produced a pistol and asked if he could engaged in a little target practice (he had also brought his son along). I felt that I had no right to tell him "No." So, I just nodded. But, this behavior told me that he was trying to keep any animal away from the area -- Larry, of course, denied that and argued to the contrary.

Ken, Lee Hales and I knew that no animal would show itself upon hearing a fire arm.

Cal Allen joined in with Larry and Larry's son in taking a few shots with the gun.

From left to right, me, Ken Gerhard (holding his Panther cut-out) and Lee Hales on the morning of the day taken to verify the size of the Mystery Cat in Larry Miller's "Carrabelle Cat" video.

The expedition team immediately knew that something was afoot and it wasn't a desire to actually find the feline although we all knew that the chances were slim that the original cat would be hanging around the area -- unless it was a housecat.

But, Ken Gerhard had conceived of a novel way to determine the actual size of the cat in Larry's film.

Ken had designed a cut-out profile of a Florida Panther to normal size for a young cat. His idea was to position the cut-out on the road adjacent to one of the landmarks seen in Larry Miller's video and then take measurements from the tree stand in which Larry had been perched at the time of the filming.

From those measurements, Ken intended to calculate the probable size of the cat in the video.

So, Ken and Lee proceeded to perform their experiment while my son, Robert and I, went off to undertake research in another area of the Tate's Hell State Forest and run over to the site where Jim Broaddus had seen his Black Florida Panther.

All this activity too place on the last day of the expedition due to the poor weather. So, the next morning we all broke camp and headed our separate ways.

Robert and I drove back to Central Florida. Me driving my car and Robert driving our RV separately and Ken and Lee in their vehicle drove back to Texas.

About a week later, Ken called me with the results of his cat calculations and had determined that the feline was no larger than a housecat. He and Lee announced their findings publicly. Larry Miller was NOT amused and had a few scathing remarks to make about their assertion.

That was to be expected.

However, Robert and I had a rather unusual experience on the way back home from the trip.

While driving down route 417 between Lakeland and Webster, Florida about 7 miles north of the Green Swamp Wildlife Management Area, a Black Florida Panther jumped out in front of my car. I slammed on the brakes to avoid hitting the animal. Robert, driving close behind in the RV had to do the same.

Shaken at what happened and what I had seen, I called

Robert on my cell phone to ask if he had seen the cat (the reader will recall that he had missed the Black Panther I had witnessed at Oscar Shearer State Park because he was sleeping in the loft of the RV at the time).

This time, however, Robert did see the cat himself.

Truth is stranger than fiction, I guess.

A few days later, I stopped in at Colt Creek State Park, south of the area where this signing occurred, and spoke to Scott Spaulding, the head ranger there. Scott and I had become friends and, when i confided the recent experience with the Black Panther, he told me that there had been a half-dozen such sighting events near the park over the past 4 years -- two of them involving the park rangers themselves.

Well, there you have it, A simple house cat, Florida Panther, Jaguarundi, Geoffroy Cat or oither cat species? As Lois observes "until somebody catches the cat, the actual species of this mysterious feline will remain a mystery."

The Wampus Cat

The Wampus cat is a fightening creature described as a large, fearsome water panther with glowing orange eyes that stalks its prey in the night.

Originating with the "Ewah" of Cherokee mythology, the Wampus Cat is said to be a manifestation of a demon. A curious woman disguised herself in the skin of a cougar to spy on the men of her tribe while they sat around a campfire telling sacred stories during a hunting trip. Women, it seems, were forbidden to hear these "man's night out tales."

Unfortunately for the female eavesdropper, she was revealed. In retribution for the sacrilege, the tribal medicine man bewitched her, transforming the woman into a half-woman, half-cat monster condemned to haunt the forests and swamps of the south for all eternity.

Some legends about the Wampus Cat say that the animal has six legs. Four of which are for running and two additional clawed forefeet for attacking its prey.

Sightings of the Wampus Cat also portray the animal as a fearsome looking bipedal animal that sneaks up on unsuspecting campers or hunters while they sleep around the campfire — ripping them to shreds. More benign accounts of attacks by the cryptid animal simply attribute decimated campsites to her wrath at people who dare venture into her domain.

In one sighting report from North Florida, a hunter was out one night with his hounds (apparently intent on poaching). Without warning, the dogs both whimpered and took off into the woods away from the game trail they were exploring.

"Then, I smelled a nasty smell, like a wet dog that had come on a polecat," said Dean Morris, the hunter. Morris heard something hiss loudly from behind him on the trail. He spun around and saw a horrible sight. Morris found himself eye to eye looking into the glowing orange orbs of a Wampus Cat. The animal had large discolored fangs that dripped with foam. "It looked kinda like a really big Florida Panther, but it walked on two legs like a man."

Scared out of his wits and with his heart beating wildly, Morris dropped his gun. The creature sneered at him which made Morris' hair stand up on end and his stomach retch.

Somehow Morris found his legs and ran in a panic through the woods with the Wampus Cat hot on his heels. Morris was able to take refuge in an old pump house with no windows and barred the door. But, he could still hear the creature panting as it paced outside waiting for Morris.

Through the night, "the thing would claw at the door and made it shake nearly off its hinges. But the door held," said the hunter. Morris spent a sleepless night in terror waiting for the door between him and the beast to give way.

As the first light of day appeared beneath the door and through cracks in the roof of the pump house, the Wampus Cat screamed in final frustration and retreated back into the woods. Morris could hear its sounds as they faded into the distance.

Finally returning home after his ordeal Morris discovered his hounds shivering, but otherwise none the worse, cowering on his front porch under a table.

In some respects sightings of this animal resemble the werewolf encounters told by folks in the American heartland,

a subject that my friend and colleague, Linda Godfrey, has researched and written about extensively.

Obviously tents and cooking gear strewn about a camp site can easily be dismissed as the after affects of a hungry bear on a rampage or the antics of marauding raccoons. But, how do you discount reports like the Morris case so easily? Fraud?

Well, the examination of the pump house revealed extremely deep gashes — like claw marks — in the outer wood surface. No blood or tissue and the wood tested negatively for biological residue when subjected to ninhydrin.

Sighting reports here are few, but From time to time, I am

sent photos along with inquiries about this beast. Some jokers occasionally try to "punk" me with photos that are supposed to "prove" that the remains of this cryptid have been discovered.

Typically the photos I receive are images of a feral House cat or wild bobcat shown without a measurement reference to indicate the actual size of the carcass.

Frankly, I privately hope that these fakers will find themselves being stalked by the real Wampus Cat one night.

El Chupacabra

Eyewitness descriptions, based on sightings, of this weird creature range from something unusual to an utterly fantastic animal. Most descriptions run the gamut between canids and felids. But some descriptions sound more like vampire bats and gargoyles than a feral dog or cat. In these reports, the Chupacabra can fly or is reportedly seen lurking on tree branches.

The Chupacabra is accused of attacking a variety of livestock and pets – killing them with puncture wounds to the throat and sucking its victim dry of blood.

When I first moved back to Florida in the late 1990s, there was much excitement one night at Grenelefe Resort where I lived for a time. Their security, a self-contained police force was called when a resident reported a "strange, red-eyed creature" stalking her dogs just outside of the complex from inside of an adjacent orange grove.

The investigating officer actually saw the creature and gave chase, so the case made it to the police blotter maintained by the Golf Resort. According to the security report, several people actually saw the "weird creature" and called it in.

On the other side of the county, a "Chupacabra" was killed on the Fussell Ranch in Green swamp in December of 2009. The strange animal was killed with a single gunshot to the head. Before he shot it, Mister Fussell thought the two animals were monkeys, because it was standing in a tree. In fairness, Fussell's thought may have been impacted by the escape of fifteen patas monkeys from a nearby property the previous year. However, all the monkeys had all been recaptured before this incident.

As with most "Chupacabra" specimens found, this one was hairless and extremely odd in appearance with a sickly bluish skin. It has a long snout and slight legs which end hand-like paws.

Fussell shot it, so he said later, "to get a better look at it." The second animal, likely the creature's mate, escaped into the woods.

"I seriously believe it might be a Chupacabra," said Paul Fussell in an interview "But you can't say for sure until you have some proof."

Florida Fish and Wildlife experts dismiss the animal as "a rare breed of dog called a Peruvian Inca Orchid." But, Dwight Fussell believes the experts are wrong. "It ain't got no feet like a dog," he said.

Before this event, while out filming an episode of the TV show MonsterQuest with producer, Troy Parkinson, videographer, Tom Phillips, and me, wildlife expert, Mark Peterson, captured an odd looking animal on a trap cam still as it checked out the bait not far from where Fussell shot his "Chupacabra."

Mark thought was some kind of wolf. I think it was a coyote. In this case, however, the animal did have some hair on its body.

Most of the time Chupacabra emails that I get shown or receive photographs about turn out to be a coyote or feral dog. As with the Wampus Cat, size references are typically omitted in this photographic "evidence." But, if there is a clear image of the animal's teeth, remains can easily be identified as those of a canid because the shape and arrangement of the teeth are a dead give-away.

Recent analysis of some unusual "Chupacabra" carcasses found in Texas have revealed that some of the reports of this creature can be written off as a hybrid of the common coyote and an odd breed of dog. Similar remains have been recovered up in the Florida panhandle.

Nevertheless, some sightings and even attacks, by the Chupacabra here are not easily dismissed as "Dogs Gone Wild."

The Cracker Dog Killer

The term "Cracker" applies to the original colonial pioneers who settled the state of Florida. It also applies to their descendants. The first wave of "Florida Crackers" arrived here in 1763 after Spain ceded Florida to England.

The root word "crack" comes from the Middle English "crack" which means "entertaining conversation," In Elizabethan English, a "cracker" was a term used to describe a brash and uncultured braggart. Although somewhat degratory, the word became associated with the old cow hands who settled Georgia and Florida, who were primarily descendants of our early pioneers.

Dogs were a common companion and pet of these cracker folk, and they had a legend about a monster they called "The Dog Killer" that preyed on their canine companions.

The monster was said to live in the hollow of trees or rotten logs. It was noted for killing overly inquisitive canines who dared to sniff around their homes. It would eat the dog and then pile its bones, along with the skulls of its victim (with those of other happless hounds) near the entrance to their lair.

Cryptid cynics will be quick to write this creature off as an alligator. However, while alligators do dig underground dens along river banks and they do attack quickly from water, they do not pile the bones of their prey near the entrance to their caves. Alligators prefer to drown their prey and stuff the body into underwater hollows until the flesh "ripens" before consuming it.

Curiosity makes for good science. Rather than scoff at reports of monsters and presume that eyewitnesses are liars with

some hidden agenda for telling their stories, it's far more fruitful to look for ways in which people may be mistaken but reporting truthfully — at least so far as they perceive the truth.

Yes, many Florida Crackers were great yarn spinners who entertained their tenderfoot guests with amusing anecdotes around the campfire at night. If you are an outdoors person that's accustomed to camping, I'm sure you recognize that this behavior is not confined to "the good old days."

So in the case of the Florida dog killer mystery we are better served by looking for a known animal out of its normal habitat or one that exhibits behavior considered outside of its normal activity. Most cryptids, after all, fall into this category and are not an undiscovered creature.

A colleague of Roland Fisch, (my mentor and friend at Florida Keys Community College), Professor Bill Smith, wrote the following note to Roland who passed the item along to me:

> *Tayra: Long-lost Legendary Cracker Dog-killer?*
>
> *One writer I read years ago was convinced he had seen the Cracker Dog Killer animal in Central America.*
>
> *The Tayra is a reasonable candidate that has been found as far north as Mexico: The Tayra is a weasel as big as a mid-sized dog. It would have little trouble dispatching most hounds. It's similar to the North American wolverine and is in the same family.*
>
> *If you find any reference to such an animal in early Florida or the other Gulf states, I'd be most appreciative of the citation.*
>
> *Thanks!*
>
> *Bill Smith*

Smith may be on to something. We've already discussed the possibility that the Black Panther, Jaguarundi and Coyote likely migrated here along the Gulf Coast. It they did, perhaps the Tayra did too. Other South and Central American animals did, at least at one time, make their home here. The Peccary, for example, once ranged in Florida.

But, there may be an even simpler answer to this mystery.

When Heather Davis, of New Port Richey, Florida, observed a dark brown otter apparently playing with her pet dog "Mike" she wasn't alarmed. The Davis family had a nice home in a fair sized piece of property with a pond in the backyard. Woods where nearby.

Mike was a friendly and inquisitive pet that seemed to have a broad smile unpleasant personality consistent with its breed. Heather hadn't noticed if Mike was initially protective or threatened the otter initially. It was more in his nature to play then to guard the family homestead.

Otters are a rather innocuous animal and rarely seem vicious. Otters are a fairly common animal in Florida and you'll see these cute and apparently cuddly creatures from time to time frolicing in the rivers and lakes here. So Heather saw no reason to fret.

But, suddenly things went sour. The four-foot-long "playmate" bit into Mike's snout and proceeded to drag the white American Eskimo into a nearby lake. When the otter started to pull the dog under, a young next-door neighbor jumped into a small boat and tried to rescue Mike by using a pole to beat off the offending otter.

Unfortunately for Mike the rescue attempt came too late.

Mike's nineteen year old would-be hero, Rick Wolf said, "The otter went under water. Then it jumped on the back of the boat and started attacking my foot." Wolf was very matter-of-fact in his rendition of the story, almost as if it were an everyday thing.

Young Heather and her sibling Stephanie, who had been hysterical during the attack, recalled later that, "The otter had its whole mouth around Wolf's shoe." Upon examination it was apparent that the shoe had not been penetrated by the otter's teeth and Wolf was uninjured.

Even after being kicked and poked by the much larger human teenager, the otter swam over to the dog's body still floating in the lake, grabbed the carcass and glided away. At this point the youngsters could do nothing but go for adult assistance.

As a rule, otters are shy and don't pose a threat to humans or their pets. But, we all know that mother animals can be exceptionally aggressive and unpredictable if they are trying to protect their litter. Of course, rabies could also have been a factor in this attack.

River otters, by the way are aquatic members of the weasel family and thus realted to both the wolverine and Tayra. Otters are found near fresh water] and their diet consists primarily of fish, but they have been known to consume birds, snakes and insects as well – which makes them an oportunistic carnivore.

The otter's intention, as to the disposition of Mike the dog, implies that it would consume the pet. Else why would the otter go after its dead carcass and fight for its possession? Nevertheless the dog's remains were found later on the bank of the pond — intact.

Otters weigh up to twenty-five pounds, have webbed toes, short stubby legs and a small, flat head. More to the point, they make their burrows near a water bank frequently under the roots or in the hollows of trees. They give birth, and rear their young, and these burrows.

Could the answer to this Florida Cryptid Creature mystery

be as simple as a case of mistaken identity? Namely the river otter like the one pictured above. Or is Bill Smith right and the more exotic explanation of a Tayra be correct?

On the other hand, could there be some unknown creature lurking among the mushu in the woods and forests just waiting for an inquisitive pet to wander a bit to close to its den?

Astor Dinosaur

Astor, Florida had its beginnings as a crossroads of sorts where old Indian and Spanish trails came together as they criss-crossed the state. The area was first explored by white men back in the late 1500s and was proclaimed an "Eden" by those few early explorers who visited its vicinity along the banks of the Saint Johns River.

Modern Astor came into its own during the era late in the Nineteenth and early Twentieth Century when small steam ships and paddle boats on Florida's interior waterways were the highways through the State before pavement and automobiles took their place. It was the time when railroads and the "Iron Horse" began to connect isolated pockets of community here.

The city's name "Astor" actually is taken from the name of the famed New York hotelier John Jacob Astor. William Astor and his family helped to settle the town (originally called "Manhattan.") and actually built a hotel there for visitors. John Jacob Astor IV, was took over his father's holdings there upon his death, but died on the Titanic before he could make contributions of his own to the town.

One of the first pioneers who settled in the area was Barney Dillard, Senior., who came to Florida as an infant in 1866. The Dillard family moved to Astor a short time later.

The young Dillard was an adventuresome sort and apparently a bit of an amateur archaeologist. He located the early Spanish mission of San Salvador de Mayaca on the east side of the Saint Johns built in 1657. He also discovered the remains of fort Antonio de Anacape constructed by the Spanish in 1680.

The senior mister Dillard also retraced the old Spanish trails that ran throughout the state connecting the east and west coasts. Among them the trail that connected old Saint Augustine, DeLeon Springs and Titusville with the Black Bear Trail that lead to Pensacola as well as the so-called "Dragoon Trail" that ran south through Lake County.

Now Dillard was apparently a pretty fair story-teller and, in his many adventure travels, picked up a fair number of legends and folktales from a variety of sources — including Native Americans and the pioneers who settled along these routes.

Sitting on his porch and around campfires at night, Dillard regaled the famous Marjorie Kinnan Rawlings, with his anecdotes and tall tales — stories that later found their way into her book, "The Yearling," which won the Pulitzer Prize for fiction in 1939 and was sometime later made into a Hollywood movie.

But, it's the Dragoon Trail that is of interest to us here. You see, "Dragoon" derives from a French word for "Dragon," one meaning of which are of course the large, fearsome

reptile that has a taste for virginal damsels left as peace offerings.

According to my friend and colleague, Adrienne Mayor, Dragons have a basis in fact. The legend of the dragon began when archaic people discovered the fossilized remains of dinosaurs. They recognized that the mineralized bones had once belonged to a living creature and tried, in their primitive way, to explain them by attributing the fossils to the monstrous creature of myth and legend.

However, dinosaurs have never lived in Florida. Sixty-five million years ago, when dinosaurs roamed the Earth, Florida was little more than a sand bar lying under shallow seawater between the Atlantic Ocean and the Gulf of Mexico.

So, why was this trail named the "Dragoon Trail?" Was it derived from Indian legends that describe an animal that had not even lived in the region before there were people to come in contact with one?

Interestingly, there are petroglyphs on rock walls in a variety of locations around the United States where ancient Native American artists rendered "dragons" which we known today as both sauropod and therapod dinosaurs.

In the swamps of West Central Africa in the Republic of the Congo, Cameroon, and Gabon there still exists, according to the natives there, a legendary creature known as the "Emela-ntouka." This cryptid animal is described as having an elephantine body, gargantuan tail, a single horn in the center of its head and rounded legs ending in feet that have three claws.

These characteristics also fit those of a ceratopsian dinosaur. Well, the Emela-ntouka of Africa apparently has, or perhaps had, an American cousin of virtually identical description here near Astor, Florida.

The "Astor Monster" so named for the town nearby where it was first sighted in 1953 by "Buck" Dillard, Barney senior's grandson. Now the young Dillard's "day job" was using the considerable local knowledge he inherited from his grandfather as a river guide, pointing the way to mullet, manatees and bird life to eco-tourists along the Saint Johns River. He is also said to have inherited his grandfather's abilities to spin an entertaining yarn or two to the delight of his tourist clients.

Buck described the beast as being about "thirty to forty feet in length, with an elephant-like gray body. large soft eyes and a scimitar horn in the center of its forehead." Buck apparently first saw the monster while walking the Dragoon Trail but later saw it swimming in the Saint Johns River and nearby Lake Astor as well. Others, primarily fishermen, verified Dillard's reports and said that they also saw the monster, or its tracks, on one of the islands within the river.

Actually, between 1955 and 1961, quite a few reports appeared in Florida newspapers. carried stories about this creature in the Saint Johns River. Most of them from anglers, many of whom were visitors and new residents of the area who were not familiar with our local lore or the nature of the characters who told it — all reporting a large animal resembling a dinosaur.

Several reports say that hunters fired their guns at the "monster" but were so startled and frightened that their shots went wild. A couple of people claimed that they heard "monstrous" sounds from some large animal obscured by the scrub palms in the jungles throughout the area.

The concentration of sightings stopped abruptly in 1961, the year before Barney Dillard, the senior, died.

Most people today dismiss the monster as a miss-identification of a manatee. These gentle sea cows do inhabit this region and are frequently seen there. However, manatees don't leave the water to walk on land. They do have grey, elephantine bodies (they are, in fact related to elephants — distantly), but they don't have a horn in the center of their head nor do they make "monstrous sounds" or have round legs ending in triple-clawed feet or a huge tail.

While a fisherman may be surprised by the sudden surfacing of a manatee near their boat, these animals are not a menacing or frightening monster.

So exactly what is, or was, the Astor Monster? No known, living animal fits the eyewitness descriptions.

Then there is that other meaning of the word "dragoon."

The "Dragoon Trail" could also refer to soldiers that are used to bully or dictate to people. "Dragoon soldiers" are military forces employed by governments, dictators and other authorities to blackjack, coerce or force people to obey their dictates.

General Hernandez, who had his base in Saint Augustine, commanded two hundred dragoon soldiers that he used to put down the famed Indian chief Osceola during the Seminole Wars from 1817 through 1858. There were encampments along the Dragoon Trail to facilitate such troop movements.

So, it's also possible that the term "Dragoon Trail" designated one of the old military pathways used to move soldiers from one place to another and didn't refer to any legendary creature after all.

Level-headed local historians and archivists believe that this explanation is the best origin for the name. I, on the other hand, being a bit of a romantic, prefer the other explanation.

You'll have to be the judge as to which explanation better suits you and Florida's Astor Monster when you visit this quaint little fishing village on the St. John's River yourself.

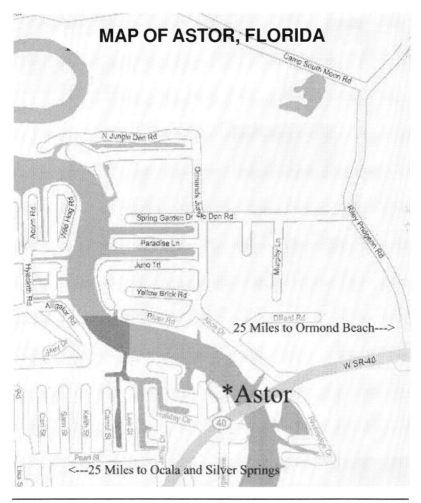

MAP OF ASTOR, FLORIDA

25 Miles to Ormond Beach--->

*Astor

<---25 Miles to Ocala and Silver Springs

The Swamp Ape

When I talk about the Florida Swamp Ape the first question I'm usually asked is about now famous photographs of a large primate with glowing eyes from behind a palm frond. The Myakka photographs that created a stir in 2000 were judged by experts to be of an orangutan.

Whether the animal was an escaped exotic or a hoax using someone's illicit pet is, as yet, unknown. However I personally lean towards the latter explanation in as much as there have been similar sighting reports in and around Tampa Bay and the Florida Panhandle for several years now.

The most recent sighting ruckus was in Glen Saint Mary's, Florida. Judging from the video taken of the animal that appeared on Jacksonville television I think it is likely that this "Swamp Ape" was also an orangutan. I Strongly doubt that the Florida Fish and Wildlife explanation of a "Orange Phase Fox Squirrel" that our wildlife "experts" tried to pass off as the culprit is unlikely.

They and I have had our disagreements before.

Then there are "mystery creature" photos that I get from time to time that purport to be of my "Big Hairy Friend." Well so far these, upon investigation, turn out to be someone trying to punk me with a phony photo like that guy in the gully suit captured by a trap cam behind a fishing camp in Lakeport, Florida at night.

Fortunately, I know the state rather well and don't waste my time, and meager resources, chasing down questionable leads. In this case a drive through the town and a short stop at a convenience store revealed that the fishing camp never existed. The photo would only fool a cryptozoology neophyte.

(The photo was not captured by a trap cam, but was copied from the website for the defunct "Freaky Links" TV show).

Nonsense like this almost always turns out to be a human in a Chewbacca of "Star Wars" fame suit or the recent Bigfoot costume sold to Matt Whitten and Rick Dyer, to "punk" Tom Biscardi, Steve Kulls, et al in the now famous "Bigfoot in a Freezer" scam. (If you are gullible enough to think that Mister Biscardi and company can be that easily fooled).

Yet, and despite misidentifications, exaggerations and outright fakes, some eyewitness reports of Swamp Ape activity do remain unexplained and are potentially genuine.

One encounter, documented by my friend, colleague and mentor Charlie Carlson is such a case.

"J.D. must have been about eighty years old when I first met him. His real name was James Dawes, but folks just called him by his initials which decades earlier, he had changed to his legal name. He was a dried up little man with tanned, leather-like hide and a prune-wrinkled face etched by years of backwoods living. I had met J.D. when I pulled into Sloan's Gas and Bait on State Road 44, just east of Cypress Lake. While filling my car, I saw him sitting there on a bench next to a bin of watermelons, drinking a bottled beer and eating one of those ready-made sandwiches. He nodded slightly as I went inside to pay for my gas. I bought a diet Pepsi and stepped outside. He was still sitting on the bench. Shoving the last morsel of sandwich into his mouth, and between chews, in a muffled tone, he asked me how much I had paid for my car. We traded a few words which grew into a drawn out conversation. Downing the rest of his beer, he wiped his whiskered chin, and went on about how he had lived in the same house since 1924. "I was raised in that place," he told me, describing a three-room cracker shack sitting on a ridge of palmetto scrub running through the Yeehatchee Swamp."

Charlie is a historian who likes to collect weird tales. He has long since discovered that anecdotes related by backwoods folks, like our friend Barney Dillard, often contain considerable color strange kind.

So, Charlie took a gamble and maneuvered his conversation with J.D. to see if J.D. "would conjure up a good story."

As is typical, until the rural folk get to know you, J.D. replied when asked about strange creatures, "Never seen one," he grinned, sliding his straw hat back on a head of gray hair, "but heard other folks talk about such things."

Charlie thought that he had had reached a dead end until J.D. added, "No Suh, never seen one. But, I'll tell you one thing. There's somethin' in that there swamp that's bothered me ever since I was a boy."

Now, *I'm* not sure what it is about Charlie Carlson that causes people to want to bare their souls. Maybe it's just that Charlie is a good listener, but J.D. opened up.

"In all of his years he had never told his story to another living soul. Now up in age, I guess he wanted to share his mind with someone willing to listen. I felt privileged that this old fellow had selected me to hear his curious tale." Says Charlie.

J.D. continued with the Reader's Digest version of his story about an astonishing event that even Charlie thought "downright unbelievable." When he finished J.D. looked Charlie straight in the eye and said, "What I've told you, so help me, is the gospel truth."

Well, J.D. had evidently hooked Charlie good with his

fascinating, but incomplete, account and Charlie (being a stickler for details) wanted to hear more. Perhaps J.D. sensed that because "He abruptly stopped, looked around and said, 'If'n you want to hear the rest (pause) you'll have to come visit for a spell.'"

Charlie was fired up and left "wanting more" in the best Gypsy Rose Lee tradition. So he quickly jotted down directions to J.D.'s residence and agreed on a day to "pay him a visit around ten-thirty on the following Saturday morning."

Charlie recalls, "On a misty Saturday morning, three days later, I pulled off route 44 and stopped beside a rusty mailbox. Through the beats of my windshield wipers I could hardly make out the fading name,"Dawes", hand painted on the side. I turned off the main highway and followed my directions down a narrow, two-rutted, dirt road about two miles paralleling the vast Yeehatchee Swamp. The morning shower had left a wet sheen on the moss draped trees along the road. As I drove up in front of J.D.'s wood-framed house I saw him sitting in a rocking chair on the porch puffing on a well-burnt pipe. Its sweet aroma drifted out to greet me. Squinting through his wire-rimmed spectacles, he stopped rocking for a moment to make sure it was me. Quickly recognizing me, he waved an invitation to his porch and offered me a seat. Other than his old rocker, the choices were limited, just a straight-back kitchen chair and an old orange crate. I claimed the straight-back chair since it offered the most comfort. I sat down and pulled up close to J.D., as I knew he was hard of hearing. The light morning rain had stopped and a few rays of sunlight were beginning to strain through the clouds. I flipped opened my writing pad, prepared to make notes about whatever he had to tell me."

As Charlie settled in, J.D. leaned back into his rocking chair and drew a couple of puffs from his pipe. Then began recalling events that took place when J.D. was a kid of nineteen years. "It was back in '26 during Prohibition when nobody could get any whiskey — except from a bootlegger. There was whiskey stills all back in them swamps. I got paid by Buck Robinson to keep a watch on his still." J.D. said, pointing in the direction of the swamp. "It was way back yonder. Down on Blackwater Creek. Ol' Robinson wanted to make sure no revenue agents came a snooping around. Hell, them moonshiners used to steal from each other. I had an old twelve gauge shotgun. One with them there single barrels, and I'd sit down there all night for fifty cents an hour. (thoughtful pause) Dadblamed skeeters! Mostly just keeping watch on things."

But during his nighttime watches, J.D. realized that something weird was also keeping an eye on him. "It was black as pitch out yonder at night — except for the fire under the sour mash boiler. A course it didn't put out much light." J.D. continued, "One night when I was out there, I kept hearing something moving 'round in the bushes. I figured it was probably a deer or bear. I wasn't feared of either of them critters, but I didn't want it to be a revenue agent either. Back then if they caught you around moonshine still they'd send you to the road gang and I didn't want that. Anyway, it was the next night when I figured out that noise I kept hearing weren't no bear or deer and it weren't no revenue man either."

J.D. paused and he turned slightly pale, "I was sittin' there, it was dark all 'round. I'd say it must've been well after midnight when I heard that sound again — like somethin' moving 'round in the palmetto bushes. But this time it let out the most god-awful moaning I ever heard. It was louder-n-hell, too. Like a howlin' kind of sound."

Charlie looked up from his tablet, "I can imagine, that must have been pretty scary for you."

Leaning forward in his rocker, JD became animated, "Damn thing near 'bout scared the devil outta me!"

Settling back, J.D. continued "Now, mind you I was out there by myself. Well, I grabbed my 'ol shotgun, stood up, and pointed it toward the woods. That moan was echoing through the whole swamp. I'll tell you, it sent shivers down my spine and here I was way out there with n'ary a soul for at least two miles. Well, after I heard that scream, whatever it was moved away back into the swamp. Then a short time later, it screamed again, like some kinda big animal, but more like a human — if'n you know what I mean."

Charlie was spellbound and J.D. who obviously an exceptional yarn spinner knew it. He would regularly go off on tangents into his family history. He also got up from his rocker periodically, saying that he needed to check on a pot of lima beans that he had been simmering all morning on his kerosene stove. You see J.D., being an old-fashioned guy, didn't have the modern convenience of electricity in his home. He in fact managed without most modern appliances.

Charlie followed him into the kitchen on one of his trips there. "Standing next to the old stove was like I had gone through some sort of a time tunnel. He was very hospitable and invited me to share a bowl of beans and a wedge of cornbread with him. Since I was getting a little hungry, I eagerly accepted and even indulged in a second helping."

When they finished, J.D. suggested, "how 'bout we go back to the porch and, sit a spell to give our bellies time to appreciate our dinner?"

By now it was mid-afternoon and warm in the heat of the summer day. J.D. hoisted a mason jar containing unfiltered well-water and took a drink. "He cleared his throat and wiped a trickle of sweat from his temple. I wanted to restart his story about the thing he had heard in the swamp. He seemed a little nervous about reliving his boyhood experience. I sensed there was more to this story and wanted him to keep going," says Charlie. Charlie prodded him, "Did you ever find out what was making that sound in the swamp?"

The two went back out on to the porch. J.D. again found his rocker and pipe. He started to fill it and settled back into the chair. There was a long, uncomfortable silence. Charlie began to fear that J.D. was having second thoughts. Suddenly, J.D. stood up, leaving the chair "rocking like a ghost was sitting in it."

J.D. went over to the edge of the porch and tapped his pipe on one of the roof support posts. "Reaching into his faded cover-alls, he pulled out a small pocket knife and began cleaning the blackened residue inside the pipe bowl. I waited patiently," said Charlie. "I'm pretty sure he was trying to decide whether to keep going or just end his story. He probably figured I would think he was nuts — or maybe making it all up."

After a while J.D. turned, shuffled back to his rocking chair, and sat down. Then, rubbing his unshaved chin as his eyes searched the woods in front of his home," as if looking for something. He turned toward me and calmly said, 'It's still out there ya know?'"

Trying to contain himself, Charlie asked, "What's still out there?" turning a page in his notepad in a vein attempt to retain his detached professional image. When Charlie told me this story later, he made a point of saying that, "I regretted not bringing a tape recorder. J.D. spoke so fast that it was difficult trying to keep up with him from that point on."

"That thing!" J.D. answered, "It's either him or one of his kind. I've been hearing him for the past several weeks. That's why I wanted to tell you about what happened to me back in the twenties."

Charlie paused a moment, looking up from his yellow writing tablet, "Are you saying that you saw whatever it was that made those moaning sounds?"

"Yep, that's a fact, sure did. It's burned into my memory like if'n you branded me with a hot iron." J.D. replied, tapping his index finger on the arm of his chair for emphasis. "When you see somethin' like that, you ain't never gonna forget it. But if'n I'd told anybody they'd a thought I was crazy as a loon."

Thinking, "So that was it." Charlie, trying to keep his poker face, mumbled "I can imagine..." as he fumbled with his pen, and prepared to record more notes. Pressing J.D. with some urgency in his voice, Charlie asked, "So, will you tell me what you saw?"

"J.D. inhaled deeply and then started telling Charlie the rest of his story."Well, about two or three nights later. I was out there at the still. You could smell the mash cooking a mile away. I think maybe the smell is what attracted this thing. He must've smelled the mash. Anyway, I was watching the still when I heard that thing moan and yell again. This time it sounded mad. I grabbed my shotgun and got the hell out of there. The hell with that still. I didn't know what that thing was and I wasn't gonna hang 'round to find out."

With a look in his eyes that told Charlie that J.D. was reliving the events, J.D. continued, "I ran down the path to where the sand road was. The road I always took out to the still in the afternoon and come back by at sunrise. So there was always daylight. But this time it was dark, there was a full moon which give a little light, but it was still pretty dark. I could make out the white sand of the road in the moonlight. At one point I stopped to listen. But, I didn't hear nothin' so I started up again."

Again, Charlie gazed up at J.D. and paused from writing long enough to ask, "Did this road go through a swamp?"

J.D. answered, "Yes sir. It was on a wide sandy ridge. Like sugar sand. There was thick swamp on both sides. I had gone pert-near half a mile or so, until I came to this curve in the road. Palmettos were purty thick in that part. I could see the road plain as day in the moonlight." At this point J.D. paled and posed to collect himself. "Then, all of a sudden, a great big, dark thing stepped out of the woods. I mean it was as close as me to you. That damn thing had to be eight feet tall if'n it was a foot. I stopped dead in my tracks. It was just standing there in the middle of the road blocking my way. My heart was going a hundred miles a minute. Listen to me, boy, when they say you CAN be scared to death. Believe me. It pert-near happened to me!"

J.D.'s story telling skills were so genuine that Charlie felt "a

quick shiver run down my back." He managed to stutter, "Wa. What was this thing? A big bear?"

With a slight laugh, J.D. exclaimed, "Hell no! This thing stood on two legs like a man. 'Cept it looked like great big monkey. It weren't no bear. I know what a bear looks like and this thing was more human, but with shaggy hair allover it, 'cept the face part. Its arms were long. They hung pert-near to the ground. I could see its eyes shining like big orange marbles in the moonlight. And, and, its mouth was opened a little. 'Nough that I could make out its teeth. It was breathing real heavy and I could see its chest going in and out every time it too wind. And did it STINK! Good Lord Almighty! Son, rotten catfish don't smell that bad. It had a musk or else it musta been wallering in pig shit 'cause it stunk to the high heavens. 'Nough to make a buzzard puke. That smell seemed to just hang thick in the air."

As a folk historian, Charlie was well aware of the Florida's version of Bigfoot, the "Skunk Ape" so when J.D.'s story began to parallel the tales he'd heard before, he had to do a "little fishing" to see if J.D. was pulling his leg. "It was time to ask the question," Charlie said. He asked, "You mentioned about a bad smell. Have you ever heard of the Florida Skunk Ape?"

"A what kind of ape? A skunk (pause) what?" replied J.D.

Charlie explained leaning forward in his chair, "Skunk Ape. Like a Bigfoot creature. People here have claimed to see them,"

J.D. thought about it as Charlie struggled to take notes while paying attention to J.D.'s body language. "Big feet? Well now, I guess it musta had big feet," answered J.D. with a quizzical look. "But I ain't never heard anything about what you're talking about. It didn't really smell much like a skunk. Smelt more like rotten cabbage or dead meat, to me."

Charlie was satisfied that J.D. "had never heard of the legendary Bigfoot. I didn't pursue the subject to prevent influencing his story."

"So, what'd you do when you came upon this thing...did you run?" inquired Charlie.

J.D. continued, "I finally got control of my thinking and pointed my shotgun straight up and fired it. I didn't want to take a chance of shooting this thing 'cause it could've been some kind of human being. So, I just fired my only shell into the air. BLAM!" After a short thoughtful pause, J.D. elaborated, "Well sir, when my gun went off, this thing let out the loudest howl I've ever heard! Then that big ol' thing high-tailed it into the swamp. It went one way and I went ta other. I ran down that sand road as fast as my scrawny young legs could carry me!"

Nervously looking towards the darkening swamp creeping in on them, Charlie asked, "Have you ever seen or heard the creature since." J.D. took another swig of well hater, wiped his mouth with the back of his hand and leaned over to Charlie, "Three or four times over the years while I was hunting. I came across his tracks a few times. Sometimes I'd catch a whiff of his stench. Then lately I've heard him several times over the past weeks. He's still out there, but he don't come up on me no more."

Charlie laid his note pad on an orange crate near his chair and watched as one of J.D.'s chickens pecked the dirt just off the porch as he pondered on another question.

Finally, Charlie asked, "This thing, whatever it is. Do you

think (pause) the one you've been hearing (pause) is the same one you saw that night as a boy?"

J.D., answered immediately "Yep, Sure is, it's him. He's gettin' old (pause) like me. I can tell his howl. Ain't as strong or scary like it used to be. He seems to move a little slower too."

J.D. rose out of his rocker and walked over to the edge of the porch and stared out into the swamp straining to catch a glimpse of the creature — like he was looking for an old friend. "Yessiree, that poor old feller is still out there some place. I sort of feel like I know him. I mean we first met on scary terms eighty years ago. We never made each other's acquaintance, if you know what I mean, but we've crossed paths a bunch of times over the years. Whatever he is, he don't scare me no more. He's just an old critter with not much time left on his clock." J.D. shuffled back to his rocking chair and sat down.

Then J.D. muttered, "He likes bacon."

Suddenly, taking notes wasn't one of Charlie's priorities. He put down his pen and pad, and then leaned in towards J.D., "Bacon? How do you know that?" Charlie asked, a bit perplexed by J.D.'s utterance. "I leave bacon out yonder on that fence post," J.D. replied pointing a shaking finger toward a section of dilapidated fence. "Every morning it's gone. I know it's him that takes it 'cause he leaves his tracks in the sand around that post."

As if on queue, far out in the woods — off to the left of the porch, Charlie heard "what sounded like a low, moanful howl."

This time, Charlie paled. "J.D. looked at me with a curious grin and nodded his head. My eyes darted back at him. "Is that the thing? Is that what you heard?"

J.D. acknowledged, "Yep. That's the ol' boy," J.D. smiled, apparently feeling vindicated that "someone else had finally heard the creature." said Charlie. "He's lettin' me know he's still around and have a visitor." said J.D.

Charlie tried to make light of his nervousness, "Maybe he wants some bacon," he said as he stood up sensing that it might be time to leave.

Charlie told me that, "I had spent all day listening to one of the strangest tales I've ever heard. As I drove the dirt road back to the main highway I kept glancing at the woods, hoping to catch a fleeting glimpse of the creature. The shadows were getting long and in the distance the setting sun looked like a big blazing orange. I stopped the car for a moment and rolled down the window. I listened for a lonely howl, but heard nothing. I rolled up the window and drove on."

From time to time, after the interview, Charlie would drive by J.D.'s place off route 44 on his way home at night or when passing through in the wee hours of morning. It stopped to listen for the sounds creature had made that day and was seldom disappointed.

On November 3, 2005, six month's after his interview with Charlie, J.D. died in his sleep. His body was found by his cousin, Jimmy Sloan, who had gone to check on him.

In the police report, it's noted that next to J.D.'s bed, on a small table, was a single yellow rose, a package of dried bacon and a note, scribbled in J.D.'s hand," It read, "For my old friend." Charlie explained to me work we thereafter.

He also said with unusual solemnity for a guy that fancies weird stuff, "Strangely, the mysterious lonely howls I heard near J.D.'s old place. I haven't heard them since."

I was the lead investigator in the Jennifer Ward sighting in 2004 outside of Lakeland, Florida. I'll get to Jennifer's story shortly. But one of the benefits of all the publicity that story received was the interesting sighting reports that I received from folks needing a friendly and sympathetic ear — like J.D. — to tell their story to.

One such letter came from Doug Tarrant.

> *I was trying to reach Jennifer's e-mail by way of the "Ledger" and Gary (the reporter) referred me to your e-mail box.*
>
> *It was an interesting encounter that Jennifer told about. I can understand her surprise at seeing the creature.*
>
> *I was born and raised in Miami Florida, and had hunted those Everglades ever since I was a kid and thought I knew of every animal and insect that lived there.*
>
> *The books say the first sighting of a Skunk Ape was in 1977, but it was in 1957 when a creature walked into my campsite and totally freaked me out.*
>
> *It was the smell of sausage on the fire that got his attention and brought him in. We stood eye ball to eyeball at less than 17 feet doing a "stare-down" for at least a minute and a half, before the creature, standing 7 foot tall*

and weighing about 350 pounds, decided that the three pistols in three shaky hands (there were three of us) might be danger and slowly turned and walked back out into the darkness.

I reported this 1957 encounter is in the "Bigfoot Case Book."

That encounter started a career of expeditions (later in the '60's) with two more encounters in the mid-section of Florida, where there was more action and sightings.

I joined up with Ramona Clark (Hibner) who is written up in a few Bigfoot books, (and I have a few honorable mentions as well) and while I chased Skunk Apes inward, Robert W. Morgan herded them my way. Gathering all this research data was sent to a young Loren Coleman for his first book in 1969. Also to a reporter, the late B. Anne Slate who worked with me, doing articles for Argosy and Fate magazines.

Back then. Loren Coleman and Robert W. Morgan were among the top researchers in this "Monster business." I have long since gotten out of the Bigfoot biz, after a few "run-in's" with other creatures in other sates. The Government prefers to cover it up. If Jennifer wants to really learn about our other Bigfoot related creatures, she needs to log on to some of the web-pages on the subject that I'm sure will answer some of her questions and enjoy the chase.

Best Regards,

Doug Tarrant

Hurricane Charley ripped through Lakeland Florida early in the morning on August 13, 2004. The storm touched off numerous tornadoes in the center of the state including two that hit Polk County. One man died here in Polk when he drove off a flooded highway and into a lake. In fact much of the low-lying land here, particularly in and around the Green Swamp, was underwater and many roads were impassable.

But life goes on. So Jennifer Ward found herself driving back home in North Lakeland with her two daughters snoozing in the backseat of her SUV headed North On Moore Road on August 14 after the storm had passed through.

As she approached the intersection of Moore and Tom Costine Road she saw what she first thought was a man crouched in a flooded drainage ditch on the left side of the road. As she neared the figure it stood up and she realized that she wasn't looking at a man.

He couldn't drive very fast as the road was still flooded from the heavy rains the storm had left behind. In fact little of the surrounding terrain remained above water.

The thing that Jennifer saw the drainage to ditch stood nearly erect with its hands positioned "like a begging puppy." It was covered with black hair except for "some white fur or skin pigment around its eyes." It did not have a prominent nose. Its body was quite muscular and "I couldn't see anything that would tell me its gender." Said Jennifer.

Unnoticed until Jennifer's vehicle was abreast of the animal, apparently cutting off its escape from whence it came,

The rendering of the Florida Swamp Ape seen by Jennifer Ward and others outside of Lakeland, Florida in 2004 by forensic artist, Matt Ellis, prepared during my investigation of the incident.

Jennifer passed by the creature slowly at a distance she estimated at "Five, maybe seven feet."

"I wasn't scared, but I was afraid for my daughters or I would've stopped," Jennifer told me in my interview with her. So I took the girls home around the corner, grabbed my camera and drove back there hoping to get a picture of it. But by then whatever it was had gone. "

Jennifer's significant other, Richard Funari, had been doing some volunteer work with Pangaea Institute for some time before the incident. Ritchie's interest was in fossils and he'd been digging up quite a few at a site in Bradenton, Florida. Neither Ritchie nor Jennifer knew at the time that I was an avid cryptozoology person.

But, Jennifer was so troubled by her sighting that Ritchie felt she needed to discuss it with someone familiar with local wildlife. So he brought her over to my home so she could tell me about the incident and see if I could shed some light on what animal she had seen.

To help or explain the animal she had witnessed she brought along two sketchbooks full of drawings that she had done her best to render the creature. I examine the drawings as she told me the story.

Of course I immediately realized that she had an encounter with what I call the "Swamp Ape" — preferring this term to the more popular "Skunk Ape" nomenclature associated with apparently hoaxed sightings in South Florida.

Knowing Ritchie and Jennifer fairly well at that time and reading Jennifer's body language and intonations as she related her story, and seeing her obsession with drawing the animal I began to ask questions about her sketches. At one point when I asked about the variations in her renditions of the creature's head, Ritchie said, "You should see the full-sized one she's drawn on the kitchen wall!"

Having been to their home I knew that they were in the middle of remodeling. Jennifer had attempted to draw the creature full-size on the rear of the wall board that has been exposed during demolition.

This was beginning to remind me of the Richard Dreyfuss character in Spielberg's "Close Encounters of the Third Kind" and I recognized that this sort of compulsive behavior was the result of significant mental trauma.

It was apparent that whatever happened Jennifer was relating her experience truthfully. And knowing her as well as I did I knew that it was unlikely that she would lie. It just isn't in her nature.

Thinking that it was unlikely that additional evidence was in hand, I started to instruct Jennifer as to keeping her experience a secret until I had had time to look into the matter. Then she informed me that she had gone looking around the area of the sighting to see if there was any trace evidence of the animal. She discovered very large and unusual tracks near the creek bed on her grandfather's property adjacent to where she had seen the animal. She took photos of the tracks.

Unfortunately, before I could make castings of these prints, another hurricane hit the area destroying this evidence. I did however find a clump of hair in the barbed wire fence that separated a horse stable from Moore Road.

Visual inspection of the photographs Jennifer took revealed that the prints were very similar in size and shape to a track from the Swamp Ape that have been taken in Ocala National Forest after a sighting in 1983 and given to the state museum in Gainesville. This track was passed on to me by Russell McCarty of the museum since cryptozoology artifacts are not part of the museum's collections mandate. Russ felt that I would put this item to better use than allowing it to gather dust in an evidence locker.

That was fortunate for this track has proven to be an archetype for a number of similar footprints found in remote places around the state.

2004 was the year for hurricanes. Two more tropical storms hit the State of Florida that year. One of the two passed through Polk County again several weeks later. The chances of discovering any additional uncontaminated physical evidence was slim.

I examined the hair sample I had retrieved from the barb wire fence under an optical microscope. Some of the items showed evidence of being cut with a sharp instrument. Not wanting to invest any of Pangea's meager resources and laboratory tests that I was sure would turn out to be inconclusive I retained the hair but declined the tests.

For weeks after Jennifer's experience, she continued to obcess over the creature. During this time forensics artist Matt Ellis made contact with me when I allowed Jennifer story to break in the Lakeland Ledger using some of Jennifer's sketches as illustrations. Matt offered to work with Jennifer to come up with a realistic rendering of the creature in the hope that a forensic reconstruction would be useful to my investigation and bring some closure for Jennifer.

I arranged a meeting and Matt set to work after extensive interviews with Jennifer. Not wanting to unduly influence Matt

I kept everyone away from him while he set to work on the project.

About a week later Matt called me to tell me he had completed the drawing. I set up a date then Ritchie, Jennifer and I drove over to Matt's house to see the finished product. Matt had the drawing covered on his drawing board when we arrived.

When we were ready Matt unveiled its creation. The look on Jennifer's face was as if the world had been lifted off her shoulders. She exclaimed, "That's it! THAT'S my animal. That's what it looked like!"

We took the finished drawing to Kinko's and made several reproductions, one of which I gave to Jennifer. We also had the large image scanned and reduced in size so it could be stored on a computer and emailed.

The next day I prepared a press release which I sent out to a number of media outlets and cryptozoology interest websites along with the scanned image.

Within days Matt's drawing went viral and I was getting calls from the media wanting to interview Jennifer. Some media tried to go around me and get in touch with Jennifer directly. But I had cautioned her not to talk to anyone and refer them to me so that her testimony would not be corrupted by improper questioning. To her credit she has stock for this procedure.

One major media outlet became abusive when I informed them that they would follow this procedure or forfeit any contact with Jennifer. They resented being told that they would have to submit their questions to me for approval in advance.

But then it got crazy. Certain Bigfoot research organizations sent "curators" to investigate Jennifer's story. They demanded access to Jennifer. Making them follow the same routine as the media I declined allowing them to talk to Jennifer because the construct of their questions with such that they were actually telling her what she saw and not eliciting a factual account.

Somehow a Georgia convict obtained Jennifer's address and sent her a note claiming to be half Bigfoot. The letter was obviously intended as a device to gain her sympathy and likely access to her bank account. I took the matter up with the warden that they pedal facility from which it originated.

Seeing that a media circus would be counterproductive to a proper scientific investigation of the sighting, Jennifer and I agreed to let the furor died down.

A couple of months later we agreed that Jennifer would appear student films on the Florida Swamp Ape. The film "Footprints" produced by students at Florida international University went on to win "Best Student Film" at the New York international film Festival.

In the meantime I conducted field research in and around the Green Swamp North of where Jennifer had her encounter. During one investigation with my cryptozoology students and my friend and colleague Ken Gerhard we discovered tracks in the vicinity of our investigation.

However we had to be on our guard as our expedition was crashed by the Bigfoot research "curators." Thanks to Ken's keen eye and my own we realized the tracks had been planted.

But, once rid of the crashers, who'd been asked to leave by the Rangers after they caused a ruckus in a drunken episode the previous night, we discovered a configuration of six apparent ground nests arranged around an odd woven branch enclosure. The nests were in a state of decay, but recognizable due to their consistent configuration of debris.

I discounted the enclosure is a natural formation due to a vortex wind, but I also concede that an animal could have used it as some sort of shelter.

The nests, on the other hand, were interesting in that they resembled nests made by the Bili Ape Africa but composed of native materials.

Each nest of base of straw pine upon which wide palm fronds were laid. Both the pine and the fronds had to have been carted in from considerable distance. On top of the palm was a layer of Spanish moss.

The later careful examination of the moss in my lab at the college revealed several black fibers which I retained pending an appropriate time for more detailed testing. Frankly, with the curators breathing down my neck, crashing scientific expeditions, ignoring forensic protocols and apparently planting bogus evidence, I was concerned that any tests I performed would be call to question.

In fact these "professionals" did resort to lame attempts at character assassination when our work began to make news. But that's another story.

Then on June 7, 2006 I was awakened at one in the morning by a phone call from Ritchie. I had just done the Crypto-Tuesday radio show with my radio partner, Ed Craft, and was spending the night in Ft. Lauderdale at an RV park there.

Ritchie and Jennifer's neighbor Down the road, Kelly Clark, and his dogs had just chased a creature up the street that was lurking near his mailbox. The dog started barking and Kelly had gone out to investigate. Kelly, who is your stereotypical country boy, lives in a trailer where Tom Costine Road has a T-.junction with Beverly Hills Road on the opposite side of Jennifer's neighborhood.

Kelly was aware of Jennifer's encounter two years previously, and despite his excitement at his own sighting remained calm enough to think clearly and contacted Ritchie who in turn was able to contact me having my private cell phone number.

The area in front of Kelly's trailer is dimly lit at night and the yards there are quite large and fenced in. There are several large trees on Kelly's property which sits above the road. The animal stood motionless, despite the barking dogs, when Kelly came out of his home. It was behind one of the trees and down on the road where Kelly could not immediately see it. As he approached, Kelly stepped on a twig which snapped and the animals took off on two legs up the road to the north.

After running by people he for about twenty paces the animal dropped to all fours and skedaddled up the pavement. Kelly could hear the nails of its hands and legs striking the macadam as it ran. By this time all the dogs in the neighborhood, which included all the adjacent yards, were barking wildly at the creature.

I arrived the next morning and started to investigate. I took Kelly's statements and those of his girlfriend who had observed the events from the bedroom window previous night on digital media. Then proceeded to search for physical evidence of the animal along the fence line across the street, by the mailbox, and North to the forested area on Tom Costine Road. But there was nothing to be had.

About two years after Kelly's sighting, Painless Productions of LA asked me if I'd do a TV show with them for the Discovery Channel. They asked if Jennifer would be available to tell her story on camera.

Figuring it was time to go national, I asked Jennifer if she was available and we agreed to do the show. My former student, and now associate, Robert Robinson, lent a hand during the filming with show host Chuck Nice. We took the crew to the site at Moore and Tom Costine Roads were Jennifer met us to do the filming.

After concluding the interview with Jennifer and Kelly, we took Chuck and crew into the Green Swamp to discuss our findings. For some reason I took the vial containing the hair sample we found — thinking that perhaps time and circumstances were right to reveal their existence.

Towards the end of the interview Chuck inquired about physical evidence found during our investigations in the area. I produced the vial from my pocket and explained how it was obtained and asked if the producers would like perform the tests. I think Chuck was a little shocked, based on his expression, and he almost gratefully accepted the sample.

The producers had Chuck take the sample to the forensics lab at USC when he returned to LA. It was examined by Dr.; Micheal Hughes, a forensic hair specialist, who determined that the fiber was indeed hair and that the animal it came from was "not a known North American species."

Imagine that!

Well, it's a long way from confirming the existence of the Swamp ape. But it's step in the right direction.

The hair sample is certainly anomalous. Its morphology is unlike that of any ape hair with which I am familiar. But let's not get too technical here.

On a recent expedition in South Florida Robert Robinson and I checked out a vocalization report I received from Richard Gilmore. Richard reported an odd howl while fishing in a pond on private land near the end of Sable Palm Road outside of Naples Florida. (Richard had permission to be fishing there).

It was about 5:30 in the morning when we approached the location from the south on a dirt road that required the abilities of Rod's four-wheel-drive jeep.

After turning around at the point where the road was blocked by a locked gate and driving a few yards back towards US 41, I told Rob to stop the Jeep and cut the engine.

We could hear the morning chorus of birds, frogs, and a small gator from behind a screen of tall reeds on each side of the road.

Suddenly off in the distance from the vicinity of the lake Gilmore had specified we heard a very strange howl. No sooner had the animal, whatever it was, called out at the rising Sun then dogs all over the rural hammocks nearby began to bark wildly.

Since our expedition plans have been disrupted the previous night with late arrivals and last-minute car problems we

Jennifer Ward's own drawing of the face of the Swamp Ape she encountered outside of Lakeland, Florida on Moore Road in 2004.

neglected to bring the parabolic microphone recorder along.

On the way in Robert Robinson had seen members of our expedition crashing "friends" filming along Route 29. Suspecting another attempt at setting us up, I wasn't concerned about the equipment and was more worried about not wasting time assigning a team to Gilmore's vocalization report.

When Rob arrived in the early hours, I didn't want to wake the crew before I had checked out the report myself. Was that ever a mistake!

For the next three days we all got up early and traipsed over to the lake area in the hope that the animal would make the vocalization again and we would be able to capture it on tape. No such luck!

Nevertheless I suspect that what we heard was the same mournful cry that Charlie Carlson, who came along as part of the team, had heard in the Swamp outside of J.D.'s home.

We may never know.

Does the Swamp Ape exist? There's more than enough circumstantial evidence to prove he does in a court of law. But that isn't the same as proving it to science.

I look forward to the day, and what I hope is not the distant future, when science is given satisfactory evidence that it, and other yet undiscovered cryptic creatures of Florida, actually do live.

Biographical Index

W

Meet the Author:
Scott Marlowe

Proclaimed as, "America's most credible ryptozoologist," Scott Marlowe, spends as much time in camos and boots as he does in a lab coat and oxfords.

A Fellow Of the famed Pangea Institute and educational consultant to the American Primate Conservation Alliance, Marlowe is the first expert in the field to succeed in establishing an on-going college course in cryptozoology at a state institution of higher learning anywhere in the world.

His cryptozoology course, hailed as one of the "Top Ten" news stories of 2004 by The Cryptozoologist, a well-known insider eMagazine, has won both accolades and awards for its fresh approach and application of forensic science methodologies to the study enigmatic animals.

Marlowe's television credits include, MonsterQuest, Is it True, Legend Hunters, Destination Truth and Weird Travels in addition to countless radio appearances, TV guest spots and lecture tours.

This book is your chance to meet the legendary cryptid animals researched by this world-class cryptozoologist in their native Florida habitats.

Made in the USA
Charleston, SC
08 March 2014